I0753076

A SHORT HISTORY

of the

SEVENTH ARMOURED DIVISION

OCTOBER 1938 TO MAY 1943

The Naval & Military Press Ltd

Published by

The Naval & Military Press Ltd
Unit 5 Riverside, Brambleside
Bellbrook Industrial Estate
Uckfield, East Sussex
TN22 1QQ England

Tel: +44 (0)1825 749494

www.naval-military-press.com
www.nmarchive.com

Contents

INTRODUCTION

Foreword

There is nobody better qualified to write the history of the 7th Armoured Division than Lt.-Col. R. M. P. Carver. Except for short periods at the Staff College and on the Staff of 30 Corps, he has served throughout the campaign with the Division. He started the war as Camp Commandant at Divisional Headquarters and later served on the "Q" Staff. He was GSO I of the Division from July, 1942 until April, 1943. He commanded the 1st Battalion, Royal Tank Regiment in the final battle at Tunis.

I am very grateful to Lt.-Col. Carver for placing on record such a clear and interesting account of the fortunes of the Division.

It is a great story built up by the work of many individuals and units. All who have shared in making this history will read it with pride. Those who still serve with the Division or who join it in the future have a reputation to uphold which we in the Division think is second to none.

G. W. E. J. ERSKINE,
Major-General,
Commander, 7th Armoured Division.

June, 1943.

Introduction

THIS History is very much E. and O.E. It is written almost entirely from personal memory and there may, therefore, be some mistakes of time and place. I do not think there are many. Some actions or periods have been dealt with at greater length than others. This is due either to the fact that I remembered them in greater detail or that they were little known. It is not meant to compete with the imaginative effusions of war correspondents. My purpose was to provide a record of the Division's doings for the many members of the Division who have not served in it since its birth. No such record would be complete without a tribute to the other Formations and Services, without whose help we could have achieved nothing. Of other Divisions, 4 Indian Division will always remain our oldest and closest friends ; 2 N.Z. Division and 1 Armoured Division have been our companions almost as long. More recently 51 (Highland) Division has been a close and constant comrade. 8 Armoured Brigade and 23 Armoured Brigade are close friends, and the Fighting French have served more often under our command than under any other Formation. We must also not forget the great work of the Australian and South African Divisions and of 1 Army Tank Brigade in the early days.

201 Guards Brigade, both the old and the new, we were always proud to command. The Royal Navy has kept us in the field and helped to keep the enemy out of it all the time. Unfortunately we never had the opportunity of knowing them well, except our old friends the Gunboats *Ladybird*, *Aphis* and *Terror*.

In the early days we knew intimately all the Royal Air Force with us. 208 (A-C) Squadron we regarded almost as a permanent part of the Division. Since then they have grown so large that we could not hope to know more than a few, of whom 40 (A-C) Squadron, S.A.A.F., 6 Squadron and 239 and 270 Wings have been well known to us.

There are so many more of all arms and services who have contributed to our story that I could not mention them all. As long as we realize that, it is enough.

I repeat that this story does not claim to be more than a record, bald and unadorned, compiled from personal memory. Errors and omissions must be forgiven.

R. M. P. CARVER,

Lieut-Colonel,

Royal Tank Regiment.

In the Field.

June, 1943.

Chapter I

MUNICH CRISIS TO THE FIRST OFFENSIVE

October 1938 to December 1940

THE 7th Armoured Division was conceived out of the Cairo Cavalry Brigade by the Munich Crisis in September, 1938. On 17th September, 1938 the following units were sent hurriedly to Mersa Matruh, there forming the Matruh Mobile Force under command of the late Brigadier H. E. Russell, then Commander, Cairo Cavalry Brigade

H.Q. Cairo Cavalry Brigade and Signals
3 Regiment, Royal Horse Artillery
7 Hussars
8 Hussars
11 Hussars
1 Batallion, Royal Tank Regiment ;
5 Company, Royal Army Service Corps
2/3 Field Ambulance.

The force was based and leaguered inside Matruh Fortress, and was to support the garrison, part British and part Egyptian, by operating in the area of Charing Cross. The equipment of the force was primæval. 3 Regiment R.H.A. had 3.7 Howitzers towed by dragons, 7 Hussars had two squadrons of light tanks varying in Marks from III to VIB, but had no .5 ammunition. 8 Hussars had Ford 15-cwt. pick-ups mounting Vickers-Berthier guns. 11 Hussars had pre-historic Rolls-Royce Armoured Cars with a few Morrises. 1 Battalion R.T.R., who had come out from England with all the light tanks in that country in March, were complete with 58 light tanks, but they had little track mileage left and the few new tracks there were would not fit. 6 Battalion R.T.R., with old mediums and lights, had been left in Cairo for internal security.

208 (A-C) Squadron equipped with Audaxes, 80 (F) Squadron with Gladiators and 45 (B) Squadron with Harts supported the force. Great excitement was caused by the arrival of a flight of Blenheims from Iraq, the first we had ever seen.

The excitement died, but at the same time Major-General P. C. S. Hobart arrived by air from England to form a Mobile Division. He was at that time DDSD (AFV) in the War Office, after having been DMT, and was, of course, well known to all as the commander of the first and only Tank Brigade from 1931 to 1935. After a few exercises we all returned to Cairo in October, where the Division was joined by 1 Battalion, King's Royal Rifle Corps, who arrived from Burma. They were commanded by the late Lieut.-General W. H. E. Gott.

General Hobart, whose command was known as "Mobile Division (Egypt) and Abbassia District," then set himself to the strenuous task of organizing from scratch the formation, training, equipment and administration of a Mobile Division to operate in the Western Desert. He had to fight a great deal of obstruction, ignorance and idleness, but his enthusiasm and determination never flagged ; and when the Division moved to Gerwala for a month's collective training in March 1939, the progress that had been made was most remarkable. Owing to the limitations on track mileage only two exercises with tanks could be carried out, and training was concentrated on B Echelon which was then Divisionalized, the whole of the Division's B Echelon amounting only to some 300 vehicles.

The Division returned again to Cairo. During the summer 7 Hussars were completed to three squadrons of light tanks and 8 Hussars began to receive two-man light tanks discarded by 7 Hussars and 6 Battalion, R.T.R. Throughout the summer discussions, conferences and exercises were held on every aspect of the Division's training and organization. When the international situation grew dark the Division moved up to Matruh and was concentrated in the area of Charing Cross. The difference between the Mobile Division of August, 1939 and the Matruh Mobile Force of September, 1938 was remarkable. There had been a few changes in equipment. 3 Regiment R.H.A. were equipped half with 37 mm. anti-tank guns, half with 25-pounders and a Battery of 4 Regiment R.H.A. was attached to the Division. They had arrived from India during the summer, had been mechanized and been equipped with 25-pounders on converted 18-pounder carriages. 11 Hussars had received some more Morris Armoured Cars, but not until October, when the first ten A-9 Cruisers reached 6 Battalion, R.T.R., was there any better tank than the Mk. VIB light. The Division was organized as follows :—

LIGHT ARMOURED BRIGADE (Brigadier H. E. Russell)

- 7 Hussars
- 8 Hussars
- 11 Hussars

HEAVY ARMOURED BRIGADE (Lt.-Col. H. R. B. Watkins, R.T.R.)

- 1 Battalion, R.T.R.
- 6 Battalion, R.T.R.

PIVOT GROUP (Lt.-Col. R. Mirrlees, R.H.A. and later Lt.-Col. W. H. E. Gott)

- 3 Regiment, R.H.A.
- F Battery, 4 Regiment, R.H.A.
- 1 Battalion, K.R.R.C.

Lt.-Col. Gott acted as GSO I, no GSO I being allowed on establishment, and Major C. M. Smith, R.A.S.C., was DAA & QMG. The improvement in training generally was great ; the most remarkable advance, however, was in the field of administration. No provision had ever been made officially in the British Army for the administration of a large mobile mechanized force in a featureless, almost waterless desert with no communications. The system of administration now generally adopted by all mobile formations in the Western Desert is based on the foundations laid by General Hobart and Major Smith in the year before the war, and later developed within the Division in the first year of the war.

War with Germany broke out and it soon became apparent that Italy had decided to sit on the fence for the moment. After a series of exercises the Division returned to Cairo in November, General Hobart leaving the Division which he had organized and trained from a unco-ordinated collection of units with no administrative organization into a fighting formation fit to take the field in spite of the paucity of its equipment.

In January, General Michael O'Moore-Creagh arrived to take over the Division, the Heavy Armoured Group became 4th Armoured Brigade and Brigadier J. A. L. Caunter arrived to command it. He had commanded 1 Battalion, R.T.R., until March, 1939, when he had gone home to take command of the newly formed 1st Army Tank Brigade. The Light Armoured Brigade changed its name again to 7th Armoured Brigade ; the unofficial Pivot Group became officially the Support Group, commanded for a short time by Colonel Williams, later by Brigadier Gott ; 2 Battalion, Rifle Brigade, arrived from Palestine, forming the second motor battalion of the group. 3 Regiment, R.H.A. were converted entirely into an Anti-Tank Regiment and 4 Regiment R.H.A., although not yet officially part of the Division, trained with it and were regarded as such.

When war with Italy became a possibility 11 Hussars and the Support Group moved up to Matruh, 11 Hussars maintaining one Squadron at Sidi Barrani with one troop on the frontier at Salum. Meanwhile the Regiments of the Armoured Brigades were reshuffled, 4 Armoured Brigade consisting of 7 Hussars and 6 Battalion R.T.R., 7 Armoured Brigade of 8 Hussars and 1 Battalion R.T.R. On May 14 the rest of the Division less 7 Armoured Brigade, moved up to Gerawla ; 7 Armoured Brigade remaining in Abbassia, 8 Hussars not yet having more than one Squadron equipped and trained. 7 Armoured Division was then the main part of Western Desert Force, formed by H.Q. 6th Division and commanded by General O'Connor. The only other troops in the force were the Cairo Infantry Brigade, garrisoning Matruh. The small air force, which included 208 (A-C) Squadron newly equipped with Lysanders, was commanded by Air Commodore Collishaw and had Gladiators and Blenheims as fighters and bombers.

On the night 10-11 June, when war against Italy was declared, 11 Hussars and Support Group moved up to the frontier followed by the rest of the Division on the following day. Support

Group took over the coast with one battalion in Salum and one in reserve at Buq Buq, 11 Hussars crossed the frontier and patrolled all round Capuzzo and 4 Armoured Brigade moved up south of the escarpment. The first engagement of the war was when 11 Hussars captured Sidi Omar, the occupants not knowing that war had been declared. The next battle was the capture of Fort Capuzzo, a dramatic scene in which those Cruisers, which were lucky enough to have guns, bombarded the walls of the fortress with 2-pounders. Throughout the summer, skirmishes took place around Capuzzo, which changed hands several times, and patrols of 11 Hussars penetrated as far as Bir Gobi and the Bardia-Tobruk road. At this time 2 (Cheshire) Field Squadron and 141 Field Park Troop joined the Division from 1 Cavalry Division. At the end of June, 7 Armoured Brigade relieved 4 Armoured Brigade in the area of Sidi Suleiman. The enemy's air force, operating as they did almost without interference, was a constant source of annoyance, particularly to armoured car patrols. Our precious handful of Gladiators had to be preserved to escort the daily sortie of the helpless Lysander Tac. R. The few tanks we had were fast wearing out and there were signs that the Italians were preparing at last for some military effort greater than the recapture of Capuzzo, which they had carried out in July, by so doing, frustrating our plan to despatch a force to capture Giarabub. The Division, less 11 Hussars and Support Group, was accordingly concentrated in the area south of Matruh, the Support Group holding the frontier, reinforced by 3 Coldstream Guards and 1 Battalion Northumberland Fusiliers. About September 15 the great Italian army rumbled slowly over the frontier down Halfaya Pass and along the coast to Sidi Barrani, harried effectively by the guns of 4 Regiment R.H.A. The Support Group withdrew to the Matruh-Siwa road, 11 Hussars maintaining contact east and south of Sidi Barrani. When it was clear, that the Italians had no intention of advancing further, having erected a monument at Sidi Barrani and announced that the trams were running again and the shops open as normal, the first of the famous Jock Columns was formed under the command of Jock Campbell, then commanding 4 Regiment R.H.A. It moved up to the area of Bir Mumin and began to worry the Italians as they extended their position southwards by the formation of perimeter camps. One column was soon followed by the rest of the Support Group, which operated one column just south of the coast road and one near Alam Mella, sending night patrols up to and into the Italian camps. 11 Hussars continued to observe the whole front from the coast to Alam Rabia. During the autumn the Division was reinforced by the arrival from home of 3 Hussars, complete with light tanks, and 2 Battalion R.T.R., complete with A-13's, thus doubling the tank strength of the Division ; also by 1 Regiment R.H.A. with 25-pounders and 106 Regiment R.H.A. with two Batteries of 2-pounder anti-tank guns and two Batteries of 20 mm. A.A. guns. In exchange we lost P and J Batteries of 3 Regiment R.H.A. to 4 Indian Division, who had recently arrived to hold the Wadi Nagamish at Gerawla. In November, 7 Battalion R.T.R. with Matildas, the first "I" tanks in the Middle East, further reinforced Western Desert Force.

The Division was now organized as follows

4 Armoured Brigade (Brigadier J. A. L. Caunter)

7 Hussars
2 Battalion R.T.R. (less one Squadron with one Squadron 3 Hussars)
6 Battalion R.T.R.
One Battery 1 Regiment R.H.A.

7 Armoured Brigade (Brigadier H. E. Russell)

3 Hussars (less one Squadron) with one Squadron 2 Battalion R.T.R.
8 Hussars
1 Battalion R.T.R.
One Battery 1 Regiment R.H.A.

Support Group (Brigadier W. H. E. Gott)

4 Regiment R.H.A.
1 Battalion K.R.R.C.
2 Battalion R.B.

Divisional Troops

11 Hussars
3 Regiment R.H.A., less two Batteries
106 Regiment R.H.A.
2 (Cheshire) Field Squadron
141 Field Park Troop
5, 58, 65 and 550 Companies, R.A.S.C.
2/3 and 3/3 Cavalry Field Ambulances
7 Armoured Division Workshops, with Recovery Section and 1, 2 and 3 Light Repair Sections.

At this time one Company 1 Battalion K.R.R.C. with one troop D Battery, 3 Regiment R.H.A. formed the garrison of Siwa, and the Premiere Compagnie d'Infanterie de Marine, the vanguard of the Free French Forces of the Western Desert, was serving with the Support Group.

Chapter II

THE FIRST OFFENSIVE AND THE SIEGE OF TOBRUK

December 1940 to November 1941

ON December 8, 1940, the Division advanced from the area of the Matruh-Siwa road to the area of what is now known as Piccadilly. Early the following morning, while 4 Indian Division and 7 Battalion R.T.R. attacked Nibeiwa,. 4 Armoured Brigade pushed through the gap between Nibeiwa and Rabia near Bir Enba, and advanced up to the coast road west of Barrani. Support Group shelled the enemy in Rabia from Wadi Senab while 7 Armoured Brigade remained in reserve between Piccadilly and Bir Enba. As soon as the success of 4 Indian Division became apparent and it was clear that the only thought of the enemy in the camps at Rabia and Sofafi was how to get out, 7 Armoured Brigade moved straight to Buq Buq. After a short action against Italian guns in the sandhills, in which one Squadron 3 Hussars suffered heavily, being caught on a salt march in front of enemy guns, acres of Italians surrendered. 4 Armoured Brigade meanwhile returned from the coast to Bir Enba and pursued the enemy along the escarpment up to the gates of Bardia, getting troops across the main road west of the perimeter. On being relieved there by Support Group, who had moved up to Salum, they returned and forced the surrender of Sidi Omar which was still holding out.

A pause ensued while 6 Australian Division was brought up from Alexandria. During this period Support Group and 11 Hussars were astride the coast road west of Bardia, 7 Armoured Brigade north of the Trigh Capuzzo between Sidi Azeiz and Gasr El Arid, 4 Armoured Brigade south-west of Capuzzo and Divisional H.Q. near Sidi Omar. 4 Indian Division having already set off for the Sudan. Shortly after Christmas Day, 6 Australian Division with 7 Battalion R.T.R. attacked Bardia, Support Group co-operating from the west. On the second day of the attack, when its final surrender was certain, 7 Armoured Brigade moved west to what was later known as Knightsbridge, and thence to Acroma, patrols cutting the road west of Tobruk. 4 Armoured Brigade followed to the area north west of El Adem and Support Group took over the Acroma area establishing itself, as at Bardia, astride the coast road west of Tobruk. 7 Armoured Brigade moved west to the area south of the escarpment at Gazala, 11 Hussars patrolling from Tmimi to Segnali. Another pause followed while 6 Australian Division and the remnants of 7 Battalion R.T.R. were brought up for the assault on Tobruk. During this period patrols were pushed forward as far as

Martuba and Mechili, the latter occupied by the enemy. As a result of mechanical troubles our tank strength had now fallen to some 50 cruisers and 50 light tanks. 8 Hussars in 7 Armoured Brigade and 6 Battalion R.T.R. in 4 Armoured Brigade were therefore dismounted and the tanks redistributed. On January 22 Tobruk was attacked, 4 Regiment R.H.A. taking part in the barrage and Support Group again co-operating from the west. On the second day of the attack, success was certain and 4 Armoured Brigade, with 3 Hussars from 7 Armoured Brigade, moved that night, arriving east of Mechili on the following day. Owing partly to lack of petrol, partly to the extreme inaccuracy of the only map, an old Italian 1-400,000, the enemy eluded our grasp and withdrew through the hills to Slonta. An abortive chase by Support Group failed to make contact, the going being very difficult and the tracks bearing no relation to the map.

Another pause followed while one Brigade of 6 Australian Division drove the enemy out of Derna and the overburdened " Q " Staff tried to catch up. 4 Armoured Brigade were then west of Mechili, 11 Hussars patrolling to the west of them, Support Group and 7 Armoured Brigade near Mechili itself and Divisional H.Q. a few miles south of the fort.

It soon became clear that the enemy did not intend to stay in the Gebel and plans were made for the Division to advance to Msus, as soon as the administrative situation allowed, in order to cut the road south of Benghazi. Air reports soon showed that the enemy had begun to leave Benghazi and it was decided to move to Msus immediately. What would now be called a Field Maintenance Centre was hurriedly formed some 30 miles south-west of Mechili in front of the leading troops, and on the morning of 5 February the whole Division advanced, 4 Armoured Brigade leading. While 4 Armoured Brigade was replenishing at the dump, we were ordered to send a force immediately to cut the coast road, the evacuation from Benghazi having already begun. A wheeled force was hurriedly organized, consisting of 11 Hussars, 2 Battalion R.B., 4 Regiment R.H.A. and one Battery 106 Regiment R.H.A., which went ahead of the rest of the Division. After 15 miles of atrocious stony ground, the going improved and the advance continued until the moon went down about one o'clock. By that time the wheeled force was halfway between Msus and Antelat, the rest of the Division being some 15 miles east of Msus. The following day the wheeled force reached the coast road south-west of Beda Fomm, just before the first column from Benghazi approached. Support Group and 7 Armoured Brigade, less 3 Hussars who were with 4 Armoured Brigade, moved on Sceleidima which was held, 4 Armoured Brigade reaching Antelat. On February 7, 4 Armoured Brigade advanced to Beda Fomm followed by 7 Armoured Brigade, while Support Group, having pushed the enemy out of Sceleidima, moved on Soluch and Ghemines. The enemy were now halted on the road and had some 60 new M-13 tanks with them these tried in vain to break through 2 Battalion R.B.'s thin green line astride the road and across to the coast, while 4 Regiment R.H.A. pounded the transport massed on the road and 4 Armoured Brigade moved up and engaged them from the east. On the morning of 8 February they made one more effort to get through, but 2 Battalion R.B. and the battery of 106 Regiment R.H.A., almost at the end of their ammunition, held fast, while 4 Armoured Brigade completed their destruction, Support Group coming in on their tail from the north.

Surrender followed ; by this time 11 Hussars were at Agedabia, whither they were closely followed by Support Group. 11 Hussars pushed on to Agheila, Support Group following to Mersa Brega and 11 Hussars sent patrols as far as Marble Arch.

There were now only 12 cruisers and 40 light tanks fit for further service. While the future was being decided we had our first taste of the German Air Force, which began to bomb and strafe daily up and down the coast road and against which we had almost no defence but dispersion. On February 18 we began to return to Cairo, 11 Hussars leading, having handed over to King's Dragoon Guards who had arrived out with 2 Armoured Division. 3 Hussars with all the light tanks we had, 6 Battalion R.T.R., equipped with captured M-13's, and 1 Regiment R.H.A. were left behind with 3 Armoured Brigade who relieved us. The Division, flushed with victory and bedecked with captured flags, arrived in Cairo on February 22.

The current belief was that we had seen the last of the desert, and everyone began studying warfare in mountainous country in which we should be restricted to roads, with visions of Greece before us.

Such hopes were not long entertained. At the beginning of April the German counter-offensive started at Agheila. 11 Hussars and part of the Support Group were rushed up to Tobruk, Brigadier Gott having flown ahead and taken over from 2 Armoured Division Support Group in Tobruk. He concentrated his force at El Adem and withdrew in contact with the enemy to Salum, where they held the enemy temporarily, later falling back to Buq Buq. 1 Regiment R.H.A. and 1 Battalion R.T.R. less one Squadron were left in Tobruk, where they remained throughout the siege. By 3 May the whole of the Division had joined Support Group on the Buq Buq-Sofafi line. An attempt in May, in which few tanks took part, was made to relieve Tobruk, but achieved no more than the recapture of Halfaya and Capuzzo. The Germans counter-attacked on 30 May and retook Halfaya. The next attempt to relieve Tobruk, the operation "Battleaxe," took place 15-20 June. The Division had some 200 tanks under command, A-9's, A-10's and A-13's in 4 and 7 Armoured Brigades and Matildas of 1 Army Tank Brigade. This was the first occasion when the Division engaged a German Armoured Division equipped with Mark III tanks and 88 mm. guns, in a full scale tank *versus* tank battle. It ended in failure, 6 Battalion R.T.R. suffering heavily at Hafid ridge, and many Matildas, which were employed in the role of cruiser tanks, breaking down before they were knocked out. Support Group gallantly held one German counter-attack, 4 Regiment R.H.A. under Lt.-Col. Campbell using their 25-pounders with great effect. After "Battleaxe," Support Group and 11 Hussars were left in the area of Sofafi, with Guards Brigade under their command at Buq Buq, while the rest of the Division withdrew to the area south of Matruh, 4 Armoured Brigade returning to the Delta to re-equip. Brigadier Gott commanded what was known as the Forward Group, holding the frontier. A lull ensued in which Support Group columns harassed the enemy, who was building defences from Halfaya to Sidi Omar. In August, 11 Hussars were relieved by 4 South African Armoured Car Regiment, fresh from triumphs in Abyssinia, who were to become almost a permanent part of the Division. At the same time 2 Regiment R.H.A., who had served with 1 Armoured Brigade in Greece, relieved 4 Regiment R.H.A. Early in September H.Q. 4 Indian Division took over the Forward Group from H.Q. Support Group, 2 Battalion R.B. having relieved 1 Battalion K.R.R.C. in that formation. At the same time General Creagh went home, handing over the Division to General Gott. Brigadier Jock Campbell took over command of Support Group. In the second half of September 11 Hussars returned to Cairo, and King's Dragoon Guards joined the Division, which then moved forward to the area between Bir Habata and Maddalena, King's Dragoon Guards observing on the general line of the frontier south of 4 S.A. Armoured Car Regiment. 4 Armoured Brigade, consisting of 8 Hussars, 3 Battalion R.T.R. and 5 Battalion R.T.R., the last two from 1 and 3 Armoured Brigades respectively, and equipped entirely with American M-3 light tanks, known then as Honeys and later as General Stuarts, came up from Cairo to train in the area of Bir Kenayis. At the end of October they joined the Division in the forward area. 7 Armoured Brigade then consisted of 7 Hussars, 2 Battalion R.T.R. and 6 Battalion R.T.R., equipped mainly with Crusaders, but still having some 20 A-10's. At the same time 11 Hussars, re-equipped with new Humber Armoured Cars, returned to the Division. Early in November 22 Armoured Brigade, which had arrived ahead of the rest of 1 Armoured Division and had been training near Amiriya, came up and joined the Division in the forward area. The organization of the Division, lined up for the Crusader operation, was as follows :—

4 Armoured Brigade Group

(Brigadier A. H. Gatehouse)

8 Hussars
3 Battalion R.T.R.
5 Battalion R.T.R.
2 Regiment R.H.A.
2 Scots Guards

Support Group

(Brigadier J. C. Campbell)

1 Battalion K.R.R.C.
2 Battalion R.B.
4 Regiment R.H.A.

7 Armoured Brigade

(Brigadier G. M. O. Davy)

7 Hussars
2 Battalion R.T.R.
6 Battalion R.T.R.

Divisional Troops

King's Dragoon Guards
11 Hussars
102 Regiment R.H.A.
(Northumberland Hussars)
Anti-Tank
1 Light A.A. Regiment
4 Field Squadron
143 Field Park Squadron

22 Armoured Brigade (Brigadier J. Scott-Cockburn)

2 Royal Gloucestershire Hussars
3 County of London Yeomanry
4 County of London Yeomanry

Chapter III

RELIEF OF TOBRUK

November 1941 to May 1942

IN the early hours of the morning of 18 November, the Division crossed the Libyan frontier once again north of Maddalena and by evening had made contact with the enemy on the general line of the Trigh El Abd. On the following day 22 Armoured Brigade engaged Ariete Division in the area of Bir Gobi, destroying 45 tanks, while 4 Armoured Brigade had a fierce but indecisive engagement at Gabr Taieb El Essem, north-west of Sheferzen. In the late afternoon 7 Armoured Brigade reached Sidi Rezegh, the Landing Ground, on which were 19 aircraft, being captured by the Divisional Commander with Commanders of 7 Armoured Brigade and Support Group. For the next four days the battle raged furiously round Sidi Rezegh to which the Support Group clung grimly, supported by 7 Armoured Brigade, whose strength fell daily until it was reduced to a handful of tanks. 4 and 22 Armoured Brigades had engaged the enemy's main tank force near Gabr Saleh on 21st and had followed it north-west, 4 Armoured Brigade engaging from the south-east near Sidi Muftah and 22 Armoured Brigade joining hands with 5 South African Brigade south-west of Sidi Rezegh.

On 23 November we suffered a setback, 5 S.A. Brigade being heavily attacked and overrun after having knocked out some 45 tanks, Support Group being withdrawn to Gabr Saleh after having suffered severe casualties.

On 24 November the enemy advanced down the Trigh El Abd from Bir Gobi and south-east from Sidi Rezegh, causing some confusion but little damage, although he passed between the Division and the F.M.C. on which it was based. A large part of the enemy's forces spent the night on the Trigh El Abd between Gabr Saleh and Sheferzen, Divisional H.Q. and Support Group passing through the enemy from north to south during the night. On 25 November the combined strength of 4 and 22 Armoured Brigades was about 50 mixed Stuarts and Crusaders. 7 Armoured Brigade was no longer operative and was sent back to Base, never to rejoin the Division. During this day 4 and 22 Armoured Brigades helped to repel two attacks on 1 S.A. Brigade which was holding an all-round defensive position at Bir Taieb El Essem, south-east of Bir Gobi, while Support Group columns harassed enemy concentrations between Sheferzen and Sidi Omar. The situation on the following day was much the same, 4 Armoured Brigade, however, being made up to 77 Stuarts and 22 Armoured Brigade to 42 Cruisers from tanks which had been recovered.

On 27th the enemy's main body began to move north towards Sidi Azeiz and thence west along Trigh Capuzzo. 4 and 22 Armoured Brigades were ordered to engage and made contact near Gasr El Arid at 14.00 hours while Support Group harried their tail. It was on this day that a convoy of 25-pounder ammunition guided by Capts. Coulson and Whitty of Divisional H.Q. and escorted by a collection of tanks, portees and armoured cars, under Major Phillips, 8 Hussars, passed through the enemy to the N.Z. Division near Belhamed.

On 28 and 29 November 4 and 22 Armoured Brigades continued to engage the main German force on the Trigh Capuzzo near Bir Chleta while Support Group, having engaged Ariete north of Gabr Saleh on 28 November, moved north and engaged the rear of the enemy on and north of Trigh Capuzzo. On 30 November 1 S.A. Brigade moved north-east to Bir Sciafsciuf, protected by 4 Armoured Brigade, in order to try and join forces with N.Z. Division, while Support Group columns continued to harass the enemy between Bir Chleta and Gambut. 1 S.A. Brigade tried to gain contact with N.Z. Division during the night 30 November-1 December, but were held up by the enemy at Point 175 on the escarpment east of Sidi Rezegh. At first light on 1 December Support Group was covering the right flank of 1 S.A. Brigade and 4 Armoured Brigade had moved up to Abiar Nbeidat on their left flank. Soon after first light the N.Z. Division, now cut off from Tobruk, were being attacked again from the west ; 4 Armoured Brigade was ordered to go to their help. Passing north of the enemy who were on the escarpment south of Sidi Rezegh, they advanced straight down between the escarpments on to the battle field of Belhamed, where they remained until N.Z. Division had withdrawn to Bir Chleta, when they returned to the protection of 1 S.A. Brigade at Nbeidat.

N.Z. Division having withdrawn during the night to Bir Gibni, the Division was withdrawn to the line of the Trigh El Abd and preparations made for a thrust in co-operation with 4 Indian Division towards El Adem. After one more attempt to get supplies to his immobile troops sitting in the defences at Halfaya and Bardia the enemy concentrated his forces between Bir Gobi and El Adem. From 4 to 6 December 11 Indian Brigade attacked the enemy position at Bir Gobi. From then on the enemy began his withdrawal, 4 Armoured Brigade being faced each day by a screen of anti-tank guns behind which the enemy tanks took cover.

On 7 December Support Group regained touch with troops of 70 Division from Tobruk and the door thus was opened. By 10 December the enemy had been driven clear of the perimeter of Tobruk and Support Group columns were in action south-west of Acroma. 22 Armoured Brigade had by this time handed over its remaining tanks to 4 Armoured Brigade, apart from one composite regiment which remained fighting with 4 Armoured Brigade.

The enemy stood for a while at Gazala and south of it, launching one savage counter-attack against 4 Indian Division. 4 Armoured Brigade turned his southern flank by advancing to Bir Temrad and he withdrew to Mechili, whither he was soon pursued. On arrival at Mechili a wheeled force consisting of Royals and 2 Battalion R.B. was sent towards Benina and was first into Benghazi. The enemy had escaped to Agedabia followed by the Division, where it was relieved by 1 Armoured Division, Support Group being the last to leave on 16 January. The whole Division was then concentrated in Cairo Area.

Many changes took place during this period at the Base. 7 Armoured Brigade (7 Hussars and 2 Battalion R.T.R. only) had already left for Burma. General Gott left the Division to command 13 Corps and was replaced by General Jock Campbell. At this time General Campbell was awarded his V.C. for his gallant action at Sidi Rezegh, Lieut. Ward Gunn, 3 Regiment R.H.A., and Rifleman Beeley, 1 Battalion K.R.R.C., receiving posthumous awards of the V.C. Brigadier Renton, who had been commanding 2 Battalion R.B. and later the Middle East O.C.T.U. took over command of the Support Group, now renamed 7 Motor Brigade, and consisting of 4 Regiment R.H.A., 2 Battalion R.B., 9 Battalion K.R.R.C. (Rangers) and 9 Battalion R.B. (Tower Hamlets), 1 Battalion K.R.R.C. becoming part of 4 Armoured Brigade. 11 Hussars left the Division and moved to 10th Army in Iraq, exchanging one desert for another.

Shortly after taking over command of the Division, General Campbell was killed in an accident near Buq Buq on his way back from a visit to General Gott. His loss was deeply felt, coming so soon after the Divisional parade at which he had been presented with his V.C. by the Commander-in-Chief, General Auchinleck. Command of the Division was taken over by General F. Messervy. General Messervy had commanded 4 Indian Division and for a time had commanded 1 Armoured Division during the absence of General Lumsden, who had been wounded as soon as he arrived near Agedabia.

At the beginning of April the Division returned to the desert and was concentrated for training in the area south-west of Sidi Azeiz. Its composition was then

4 Armoured Brigade	7 Motor Brigade	Divisional Troops
1 Regiment R.H.A.	4 Regiment R.H.A.	King's Dragoon Guards
8 Hussars	9 Battalion K.R.R.C.	102 (N.H.) Anti-Tank Regiment, R.H.A.
3 Battalion R.T.R.	2 Battalion R.B.	15 Light A.A. Regiment
5 Battalion R.T.R.	9 Battalion R.B.	4 Field Squadron
1 Battalion K.R.R.C.		143 Field Park Squadron

Soon after arrival in the desert, General Gatehouse left 4 Armoured Brigade to command 10 Armoured Division, Brigadier G. W Richards taking over command. Brigadier Richards had been GSO I of the Division and later second-in-command of 22 Armoured Brigade. After a few weeks' training the Division moved up to the area south-west of El Adem, relieving 1 Armoured Division. During this period 4 Armoured Brigade was concentrated between El Adem and Bir Hacheim, continuing its training. The Brigade was now equipped with General Grant tanks, mounting a 75 mm. gun, each Armoured Regiment having 24 Grants and 20 Stuarts. 7 Motor Brigade, with King's Dragoon Guards and 4 S.A. Armoured Car Regiment, maintained contact and harassed the enemy between the Trigh Capuzzo east of Segnali and " F Route " where it crossed the Wadi Mra.

Chapter IV

TOBRUK TO EL ALAMEIN

May to October 1942

ON 26 May, 1942 Divisional Headquarters was situated at Bir Buid which lies 15 miles east of Bir Hacheim. The Division had under command 4 Armoured Brigade, 7 Motor Brigade, 1 Free French Brigade, 29 Indian Infantry Brigade, 3 Indian Motor Brigade. 1 Free French Brigade consisted of three battalions with some artillery, but no 25-pounders and no 40 mm. Bofors guns and very few wireless sets. 3 Indian Motor Brigade had approximately 120 carriers of which 40 arrived with them on the evening of 26 May and the other 60 on the morning of 27 were half way between El Adem and Bir Hacheim. With the 60 were 14 " I " tanks under command of Major Roberts of 4 Battalion R.T.R.

7 Motor Brigade was operating Jock Columns consisting of approximately a battery of guns and a company of infantry in the area of Segnali and west of Tengeder. 4 Armoured Brigade was in a position of readiness north-east of Bir Buid. The remainder of 7 Motor Brigade not in columns was preparing a position at Retma. The Armoured Car Regiments under command were King's Dragoon Guards and 4 S.A. Armoured Car Regiment. On the afternoon of 26 May the enemy began his advance eastward, pushing out strong advance guards of tanks. He was harassed until last light by 7 Motor Brigade who withdrew before him towards Retma. The 4 S.A. Armoured Car Regiment reported his movements during during the night. At approximately 05.00 hours, 27 May, 4 Armoured Brigade received orders by telephone to take up their southern battle position.

At 08.00 hours 27 May, 4 Armoured Brigade was engaging the enemy armour before having reached their southern battle position. Divisional headquarters was attacked and overrun by eight-wheeled armoured cars and shelled by 75 mm. guns. ACV 1, ACV 5 and the CRA's charger were knocked out. General Messervy, Brigadier S. Williams, CRA, Lt.-Col. H. E. Pyman (GSO I), Major J. A. Richardson (GSO II) and Capt. D. G. R. Reid (GSO III Operations) were captured. Major P. Hobbs (BMRA) and Capt. C. S. Elliot (Staff Captain " Q ") were killed. Numerous other ranks were killed, wounded and captured. The remaining vehicles of Main Headquarters under command of O.C. Divisional Signals withdrew to Hagfeten Nezha. The enemy pursued and the headquarters had again to withdraw, this time to the area south of Gambut, handing over command to 30 Corps.

During the night 27-28 May, General Messervy, Col. Pyman, Major Richardson and Capt. Reid escaped and rejoined the Divisional Headquarters where they had reassembled in area B 599, square 4140.

The 1 Free French Brigade had withstood the initial attacks and was in good heart within the Bir Hacheim defences. 3 Indian Motor Brigade had been overrun. The 29 Infantry Brigade, which was on the ground at Bir Gobi, had been passed by and was untouched. Retma had been overrun and 7 Motor Brigade spent most of the 28th reforming in the area south of Bir Gobi. 29 Indian Infantry Brigade was withdrawn to El Adem, and 7 Motor Brigade started operating columns against the enemy's southern flank. The 1 Free French Brigade withstood repeated ground attacks and suffered many air attacks between then and 10 June. It was decided to evacuate Hacheim on the night 10-11 June at 23.30 hours. This took place quite successfully and the greater part of the garrison withdrew. 4 Armoured Brigade was occupied in engaging the enemy in the area of Knightsbridge.

On 1 June, 7 Motor Brigade sent columns round west of Hacheim and north to Mteifel and harassed the enemy's Line of Communication which went through the gap in our main belt of minefields. They had some very successful shooting, but suffered heavily from air attacks. The enemy started to use our minefields as protection for forming-up or assembly areas between his main gap and Hacheim. It was decided therefore to withdraw the columns operating at Rotunda Mteifel and use them to relieve the pressure on Hacheim defences. About 2 June two small columns were formed from 29 Indian Infantry Brigade called " HAM " and " EGGS ", consisting of a troop of Field Artillery and a company of infantry each under command of Col. Howard Vyse, R.A. These operated with good effect westward against the enemy between El Adem and Hacheim until El Adem was evacuated on the night 16-17 June.

During the period 28 May to 16 June, Divisional Headquarters was always in the El Adem area, frequently having to move owing to enemy action.

On 17 June, 4 Armoured Brigade were engaged by a large enemy armoured force in the area west of Sidi Rezegh, lost several tanks and were forced to withdraw south. On the same evening the little columns Ham and Eggs took a wide sweep east and entered Tobruk by the main road which was still open. 4 Armoured Brigade was then withdrawn right back and behind the frontier to reform and 7 Armoured Division continued to operate with 7 Motor Brigade and fight a delaying action back towards the frontier. The enemy entered Tobruk on 20 June.

From the frontier to El Alamein the intention was for 69 Infantry Brigade to fight a rearguard action on the main road with 7 Armoured Division on the southern flank, the infantry brigade withdrawing in bounds as the Armoured Division withdrew in the desert.

7 Motor Brigade and 3 Indian Motor Brigade operated west and north-west against the enemy who were advancing down the Trigh Capuzzo. When the enemy pushed the columns back with tanks, 7 Motor Brigade and 3 Indian Motor Brigade withdrew east of the wire.

At this time General Messervy was succeeded in command of the Division by Major-General J. M. L. Renton, commander of 7 Motor Brigade. Viscount Garmoyle, commanding 2 Battalion R.B., took over 7 Motor Brigade.

7 Armoured Division in the desert, 50 Division on the road withdrew east delaying the enemy. On arriving east of the Siwa Track, troops under command were handed over to 1 Armoured Division. H.Q. 7 Armoured Division went back to the El Alamein line and took up position in the southern sector. 7 Motor Brigade, King's Dragoon Guards, 4 S.A. Armoured Car Regiment came under command on their arrival in the area of Abu Dweis.

Owing to an enemy attack on 18 Indian Infantry Brigade it became necessary to withdraw 2 N.Z. Division and 5 Indian Division who were in Qattara and Abu Dweis respectively. 2 N.Z. Division took up the position which they held all the following months with 7 Armoured Division operating on their southern flank.

On the night 21-22 July, 69 Brigade put in a silent attack on Taqa Plateau. This met with only limited success, and as there were no fresh troops, it was decided not to press home the attack further and cause unnecessary casualties.

A belt of mines was laid stretching from Himeimat north to the 2 N.Z. Division position, which was thickened and elaborated in the following weeks.

7 Motor Brigade co-operated in the series of battles at the end of July in the area of Ruweisat ridge which finally stopped the enemy's advance. It was in one of these actions that Brigadier Viscount Garmoyle was killed. Lt.-Col. Bosvile, then commanding 1 Battalion R.B. in 1 Armoured Division, took over command of the 7 Motor Brigade.

Two attempts were made at the end of July at a counter-offensive to dislodge the enemy whose tank strength was then very low. The first by the N.Z. Division and the newly arrived 23 Armoured Brigade of 8 Armoured Division, the latter equipped entirely with Valentines, along the Ruweisat ridge. The second by 9 Australian Division, 69 Infantry Brigade and 2 Armoured Brigade on the Miteiriya ridge south-west of El Alamein. Neither was successful in achieving more than local advances.

August saw the beginning of a static period. The Division held the front from the south flank of 2 N.Z. Division on the Bare Ridge down to Himeimat with patrols as far south as the oasis of Maghra. 4 Armoured Brigade, reformed as a Light Armoured Brigade, rejoined the Division, as did the reconstituted 22 Armoured Brigade which had all the tanks of Eighth Army apart from the Valentines of 23 Armoured Brigade and the Stuarts of 4 Light Armoured Brigade. The order of battle was then

4 LIGHT ARMOURED BRIGADE (Brigadier W G. Carr)

3 Regiment R.H.A.
4 Hussars with one Squadron 8 Hussars (all Stuarts)
H.Q. and one Squadron 3 County of London Yeomanry
11 Hussars
12 Lancers
1 Battalion K.R.R.C.

22 ARMOURED BRIGADE (Brigadier G. P. B. Roberts)

1 Regiment R.H.A.
104 Regiment R.H.A.
Greys
1 Battalion R.T.R.
5 Battalion R.T.R.
4 County of London Yeomanry less one Squadron, with one Squadron 3 County of London Yeomanry
1 Battalion R.B.

7 MOTOR BRIGADE (Brigadier T J. Bosvile)

4 Regiment R.H.A.
Composite Crusader Regiment 2 Armoured Brigade
2 Battalion R.B.
7 Battalion R.B. (from 23 Armoured Brigade)
9 Battalion R.B.

DIVISIONAL TROOPS

King's Dragoon Guards
4 Field Squadron
143 Field Park Squadron

7 Motor Brigade held the line of the minefield from Bare Ridge to the southern edge of Deir El Munassib, King's Dragoon Guards observing on their front ; 4 Light Armoured Brigade held Himeimat with 1 Battalion K.R.R.C., 12 Lancers and then 11 Hussars observing from north of Himeimat to Maghra, sending occasional patrols as far afield as Qara oasis. 22 Armoured Brigade were in reserve east of 7 Motor Brigade.

During August there was little activity apart from mining, until the enemy launched a fresh attack on the last day of the month. During the night 31 August-1 September he advanced from the area of Gebel Kalakh in two columns, one on the front of 7 Motor Brigade and one north of Himeimat. Considerable casualties were inflicted on him as he tried to penetrate the minefield, which he succeeded in doing in the early hours of the morning about 3 miles north of Himeimat. 1 Battalion K.R.R.C. fought a brilliant withdrawal action from Himeimat to Samaket Gaballa, supported by 4-8 Hussars. A large force of enemy tanks moved slowly east during the morning, forcing 7 Motor Brigade to withdraw as they were outflanked to the south. By the end of the day the enemy had reached the east end of Deir el Ragil and had forced 4 Light Armoured Brigade to withdraw from Samaket Gaballa. On the following day the enemy turned north-east and came to a halt with his head in contact with the battle positions of 22 Armoured Brigade and 10 Armoured Division.

Throughout the following days the enemy was effectively harassed from the east by 7 Motor Brigade and from the south by 4 Light Armoured Brigade, while the N.Z. Division counter-attacked 90 Light Division south from Bare Ridge. The enemy sat facing the Alam Hamza position, which was occupied by the newly arrived 44 Division, under the concentrated fire of the whole Corps, while the R.A.F. kept up a continuous pounding by day and night. The enemy was suprised by the effective delay imposed by the Division and the strength of force and concentrated fire he met south-west of Alam Hamza. After suffering considerable casualties in Mechanical Transport, he withdrew to a line running south-east from Qattara to the west end of Deir el Munassib, thence south to Himeimat which he held. The Division kept up pressure on him and settled down again to static conditions.

In the static period that followed, many changes took place. Major General A. F. Harding took over command of the Division from General Renton who went home, after nearly 20 years' service abroad. General Harding was an old friend of the Division, having been Brigadier General Staff to Generals O'Connor, Wilson, Neame, Beresford-Pierse and Godwin-Austen, who had successively commanded the original Corps of the Western Desert, whether known as Western Desert Force, Cyrenaica Command or 13 Corps. When General Gott took over command of 13 Corps, General Harding went to G.H.Q. as Director of Military Training and later became Deputy Chief of General Staff. It was not long before his lively personality was impressed on all ranks of the Division.

A great blow was the departure of 7 Motor Brigade, who went to 1 Armoured Division, taking the place of 201 Guards Brigade, who had been left behind in Tobruk. Three of its commanders had commanded the Division and the Brigade H.Q., 2 Battalion R.B. and 4 Regiment R.H.A. were among the oldest units of the Division. At the same time 2 Derby Yeomanry relieved 12 Lancers as the second armoured car regiment of 4 Light Armoured Brigade, and the Household Cavalry Regiment later relieved King's Dragoon Guards as Divisional Armoured Car Regiment. 1 Regiment R.H.A. and 104 Regiment R.H.A. also went from 22 Armoured Brigade to the new 10 Corps, being replaced by 4 Field Regiment and 97 Field Regiment (Kent Yeomanry). Divisional Anti-tank Regiments were reformed, the practice of having one Anti-tank Battery as part of a R.H.A. or Field Regiment being abandoned, and instead of the Northumberland Hussars (102 Anti-tank Regiment), the Divisional Anti-tank Regiment became Norfolk Yeomanry (65 Anti-tank Regiment), two of whose Batteries were already with us. A second Field Squadron (21) was also added. The Division also had under command 44 Division Reconnaissance Regiment, specially organised as a complete carrier regiment for the assault on a minefield. The order of battle in October was :—

4 Light Armoured Brigade (Brigadier M. G. Roddick).

3 Regiment R.H.A.
Greys
4 Hussars with one Squadron 8 Hussars
11 Hussars
2 Derby Yeomanry
1 Battalion K.R.R.C.

22 ARMOURED BRIGADE (Brigadier G. P. B. Roberts)

1 Battalion R.T.R.
5 Battalion R.T.R.
4 County of London Yeomanry
4 Field Regiment
97 Field Regiment (Kent Yeomanry)
1 Battalion R.B.

DIVISIONAL TROOPS

Household Cavalry Regiment
3 Field Regiment
65 Anti-tank Regiment (Norfolk Yeomanry)
15 Light A.A. Regiment
4 Field Squadron
21 Field Squadron
143 Field Park Squadron
44 Division Reconnaissance Regiment

During this period too, Brigadier R. Mews became C.R.A. in place of Brigadier G. B. Vaughan-Hughes and Lt.-Col. H. H. Withers became C.R.E. in place of Lt.-Col. P. A. Clauson, who went to 10 Corps as C.E. Lt.-Col. S. A. Maxwell succeeded Lt.-Col. H. N. Crawford in command of the Divisional Signals. In Lt.-Col. Crawford the Division lost an old friend, who had been Adjutant of the Divisional Signals when it was first formed. Lt.-Col. J. G. Cowley, who had done great work as A.A. and Q.M.G. since April, also left, being succeeded by Lt.-Col. C. E. F. Turner.

The First Fighting French Flying Column, a small mobile force including 16 Crusader tanks, was operating under 4 Light Armoured Brigade and in the middle of October the whole of the 1 Fighting French Brigade, under General Koenig, came under command and took over the area between Samaket Gaballa and Himeimat from 4 Light Armoured Brigade. 44 Division took over the area between Bare Ridge and Himeimat, previously held by 7 Motor Brigade, and carried out a series of minor operations in the area of Deir El Munassib.

Chapter V

EL ALAMEIN TO TRIPOLI

October 1942 to January 1943

THE main task of the 7th Armoured Division in the great battle of El Alamein which began on October 23 was to contain 21 Panzer Division in the south. This was done by an attempt to penetrate the minefields immediately north of Himeimat and to capture Himeimat itself and the escarpment immediately west of it. 22 Armoured Brigade with 44 Divisional Reconnaissance Regiment were given the task of penetrating the minefields, supported by the Divisional Artillery and the Artillery of 44 Division, who were to take over the minefield gaps as soon as made. 1 Free French Brigade were given the task of capturing Himeimat. The operations began with a barrage opening at the same moment as that of the main battle in the north, the advance to the start line taking place on lighted routes, cleared and marked beforehand. For clearing mines the Division had the help of three scorpions, this being the first time they had been used in action.

Our penetration of the first minefield, January, was impeded by soft going on the eastern edge and by damaged vehicles blocking the narrow gaps. By 23.30 hours the most southerly gap had been cleared, but considerable small arms, anti-tank and mortar fire was encountered from the enemy positions just west of the minefield and the gap became blocked. Supported by Machine guns, however, 44 Reconnaissance Regiment and 1 Battalion R.B. had forced No. 2 gap, 1,000 yards further north by 01.30 hours, and half an hour later the light squadron of the Royal Scots Greys had passed through and turned south west, over-running the enemy F.D.L's. and taking prisoners. By 03.00 hours a bridgehead had been formed west of the minefield, although the northern gap was still not cleared. This bridgehead was extended to about 1,000 yards radius, overrunning at least one Battalion of Folgore Division. The northern gap was then cleared and part of a Battalion of 131 (Queens) Brigade passed through, after having been held up on the west edge of the minefield.

The 1 Free French Brigade succeeded in reaching their objective just before first light, but were counter-attacked by 10 German tanks at first light. Owing to the very soft sand they had not been able to get anti-tank guns forward and were driven off the top of the hill into the open plain of soft sand below. They suffered a number of casualties, Colonel Amilakvari unfortunately being killed, and became considerably disorganised. Meanwhile, the bridgehead between January and February minefields was extended, and by 08.45 hours on 24 October 1 Battalion R.B. had cleared a further 1,500 yards southwards between the minefields. By this time enemy field and medium guns had concentrated on the area of the bridgehead, which was very congested ; life there was by no means pleasant. By 09.40 hours the forward troops of 22 Armoured Brigade had reached the eastern edge of February and the rest of the day was spent in clearing the area between January and February. In the evening about 30 German tanks approached from the north west and, moving down the west edge of February, engaged our tanks. Two were hit by our anti-tank guns, but the action was inconclusive, the enemy tanks remaining hull down, west of February at last light.

At 22.30 hours on the night 24-25 October, two Battalions of 131 (Queens) Brigade attacked February and reached a point about 800 yards on the far side. Here they met heavy small arms and artillery fire and were pinned down throughout the day of 25 October. The Divisional R.E. following them cleared an extension to the original minefield under heavy fire and the light squadron of 4 County of London Yeomanry entered the gap. They were engaged by anti-tank guns including 88 mm. from the flanks of the gap and by tanks from the far side of the minefield. Some progress was made, but the leading tanks ran on to unmarked mines about 350 yards west of the cleared gap. Several tanks were knocked out and they were unable to force the gap by first light.

By 09.00 hours 25 October, the enemy tanks had withdrawn some 2,000 yards leaving their infantry dug in west of February. Activity during the day was limited to artillery fire, mostly counter-battery, except for a reconnaissance by 4-8 Hussars on the front of 44 Division, in which several tanks ran on to unmarked mines.

During the night of 25-26 October 131 (Queens) Brigade withdrew to the eastern edge of February, where they were relieved by 132 Brigade also from 44 Division. 22 Armoured Brigade withdrew to positions supporting them. During the day of 26 October there was little activity. Enemy patrols of 3 or 4 tanks operated in support of their infantry and 30 tanks were seen in Deir Alinda. During the night of 26-27 October engineers cleared three gaps in February with little opposition and some tanks were recovered.

27 October was again a quiet day. It had now been decided not to continue the efforts to break through north of Himeimat. 44 Division took over responsibility for the front, supported by 4 Light Armoured Brigade who also took over the left flank, observing it with the Household Cavalry Regiment. Royal Scots Greys and 4-8 Hussars, all under command 4 Light Armoured Brigade, relieved 22 Armoured Brigade which was withdrawn to the area it had occupied before the battle, east of the May minefield. On 1 November the Division was moved north into Army reserve in the area of El Imayid station, where it was joined by 131 (Queens) Brigade who have remained its lorried Infantry Brigade ever since. 4 Light Armoured Brigade, with 3 Regiment R.H.A., Royal Scots Greys, 4-8 Hussars, Household Cavalry Regiment and 2 Derby Yeomanry, remained in the south, coming direct under command of 13 Corps. 44 Reconnaissance Regiment reverted to command of 44 Division.

During the day of 2 November the Division wormed its way gradually forward along the congested tracks which led to the bulge south of Tel el Eisa, where the final attempt at a breakthrough was being made. Here the Division came under the command of 10 Corps. 22 Armoured Brigade led, prepared to exploit the success of the leading Divisions, 2 N.Z. Division and 1 Armoured Division. During the night of 2-3 November, 2 N.Z. Division attacked successfully, 9 Armoured Brigade forming the bridgehead through which 1 Armoured Division began to pass. During the day of 3 November, 1 Armoured Division were heavily engaged in the area of Tel el Aqqaqir, on the line of the track and telephone lines running south from Sidi Abd el Rahman. 22 Armoured Brigade and 11 Hussars passed through the last minefield by last light and were going to advance south-west during the night to outflank the enemy in the area of Tel el Aqqaqir. There was a very soft patch of sand in their path, but this they managed to negotiate. Further progress was, however, prevented by several barrages laid on by 30 Corps which 10 Corps could not prevent. These were designed to lead and support the Highland Division and 4 Indian Division on to objectives which it is doubtful if the enemy ever held. General Harding fumed at the delay and was off at first light with a rush. Little resistance was met until the leading troops of 22 Armoured Brigade came up against the enemy in position on a ridge some 10 miles south-west of Tel el Aqqaqir, just east of Sawani Samalus. It was the usual line of tanks and anti-tank guns, the majority of tanks being Italian M-13's. While the 22 Armoured Brigade reconnoitred and engaged this position, the remainder of the Division threaded its way through the mass of vehicles in the area of the minefield gaps. The fire fight continued until last light, by which time the Queens Brigade were clear of the minefield and the whole Division was concentrated close behind 22 Armoured Brigade. 1 Armoured Division were engaged with the German rearguard to the north of us. During the day 2 N.Z. Division with 4 Light Armoured Brigade under command, had passed to the left of us directed on Fuka and by last light were in touch with the left of our leading troops, where 4 S.A. Armoured Car Regiment were raking in crowds of Italian prisoners. 10 Armoured Division had also shaken itself free of the minefields and were on our left rear. The result of 22 Armoured Brigade's battle was 19 enemy tanks knocked out and a large number of field and anti-tank guns destroyed or abandoned. The Division's objective for 5 November was Daba, 1 Armoured Division being directed on Ghazal Station, whence they were to turn west on Daba, 2 N.Z. Division on Fuka and 10 Armoured Division to cut the road west of Daba. No opposition was met until close to Daba itself, where a German rearguard was encountered. By midday both 1 and 10 Armoured Divisions had closed in on Daba from both sides and there was not room for all three Divisions. We were then ordered to make for the aerodromes on the top of the escarpment between Bagush and Qasaba, to the west of 2 N.Z. Division. To cross the escarpment and avoid the tufty country near the coast, 11 Hussars and 22 Armoured Brigade had to move south-west again before turning west. Divisional H.Q. and the Queens Brigade had not gone so far north and could take a more direct course. There were reports of large enemy columns moving west parallel to us and further south at this time. In the late afternoon 11 Hussars and 22 Armoured Brigade caught up 2 N.Z. Division who were engaging an enemy rearguard on the top of the escarpment south of Fuka. Some delay was caused here, first by having to pass through and across the N.Z. Division and secondly by a minefield which proved to be a dummy, and which had in fact been laid by 1 S.A. Division during the withdrawal in June. The Division leaguered for the night with 11 Hussars and 22 Armoured Brigade,

Divisional H.Q. and the Queens Brigade in the middle of 2 N.Z. Division. At first light the advance was resumed, some confusion being caused by a party from a German reconnaissance unit which had got mixed up in the A Echelon of the 22 Armoured Brigade, capturing and trying to get away with some petrol lorries. The situation was cleared up after an engagement in which Divisional H.Q. took part. Throughout this day, 6 November, and succeeding days small bodies of the enemy were met in the most unexpected places. At about 10.00 hours 22 Armoured Brigade came up against the usual screen of tanks and anti-tank guns stretching south and south-west from the escarpment south of Qasaba. The administrative situation now began to take a controlling hand for the first time for many months. We had advanced about 70 miles as the crow flies, but actually covered 120 miles altogether, in two days. B Echelon and 2nd Line had had great difficulty in forcing their way through the mass of vehicles between El Alamein and the minefield gaps ; added to that half the A Echelon of 5 Battalion R.T.R. and the B Echelon of 11 Hussars had been captured or dispersed. Further progress was not possible until 22 Armoured Brigade had refuelled. At the same time we were ordered to hand over all petrol to 22 Armoured Brigade who were stationary beside us. Luckily their petrol reached them before ours had been diverted. To the delay caused by this, 90 Light Division owed their escape into Matruh. Refuelling took place about midday and at 14.00 hours 22 Armoured Brigade began to engage what we discovered later was 21 Panzer Division. As soon as the battle began it started to rain. This helped us, as it enabled us to close and did not give the enemy the advantage of the light. While 22 Armoured Brigade were engaging the enemy, the Queens Brigade moved north to the east of them to occupy the landing grounds which were our objective. Owing to a miscalculation of distance they began to motor into the battle but were diverted in time by General Harding himself. The rain increased in intensity and the ground soon became very boggy, greatly hindering the movement of the Queens. The battle lasted until dark when the Division leaguered just east of the battlefield. The enemy's losses were some 20 German tanks and a large number of guns destroyed or abandoned. The rain continued throughout the night and part of the following morning, 7 November. The Queens Brigade were almost completely immobilized and 22 Armoured Brigade had to use their tanks to tow their guns and wheeled vehicles to drier ground. B Echelon and 2nd Line could see each other, but could not replenish as the lorries all got stuck in the ground between. It was not therefore until late in the day that the advance was resumed, and even then the Queens Brigade could not move. By this time leading troops of 1 Armoured Division had reached Charing Cross, but the main body was held up for lack of petrol near Bir Khalda. The Division, less the Queens Brigade, spent the night 7-8 November near El Bueib astride the track from Gerawla to Bir Khalda. Our objective was now Capuzzo, 180 miles on. The route chosen was to Bir Gellaz and then due west to the frontier. This gave us the best going, with only one bad stony patch for about 10 miles west of the Matruh-Siwa track. No enemy were met and by last light the Division, less the Queens Brigade, were some 20 miles west of Bir Gellaz. The distance we covered was again limited by the time it would take for the petrol to catch up. The Queens Brigade began to move again on this day, 8 November, but they had a lot of ground to make up and this was their first experience of moving over the open desert. Petrol was the only limiting factor to the distance covered.

The night 9-10 November was spent near Bir Khamsa and the night 10-11 November near the frontier, where the enemy's air force bombed us for the first time for several weeks. The first enemy troops were met again west of Scheferzen on the evening of 11 November. 22 Armoured Brigade turned north after crossing the frontier and at 09.00 hours, 12 November, reached the area between Sidi Azeiz and Capuzzo, at the same time as 2 N.Z. Division reached the head of Halfaya Pass. A rearguard of anti-tank guns and a few tanks was holding the line of the railway west of Capuzzo. These withdrew after being engaged, a train of one engine and a few trucks running the gauntlet of the Brigade's fire at breakneck speed. This rearguard managed to delay us long enough to prevent our cutting off the troops withdrawing west from Bardia along the coast road, although 11 Hussars and 1 Battalion R.T.R. destroyed several vehicles of the tail, after negotiating the escarpment at Menastir and Baheira. 1 Battalion R.B. entered Bardia in the afternoon just ahead of 2 N.Z. Division.

The pursuit could not be continued immediately for administrative and maintenance reasons. We had come far and fast, and most of 22 Armoured Brigade's tanks were well past their overhaul mileage before the battle of El Alamein started. The Division therefore concentrated west of Sidi Azeiz, where 4 Light Armoured Brigade returned to our command, and spent the night 12-13 November there. We were told that only 4 Light Armoured Brigade would continue to pursue the enemy, but after General Lumsden, Commander 10 Corps, had arrived and conferred with General Harding on the morning of 13 November, it was decided to continue the advance to Tobruk. 4 Light Armoured Brigade were already directed to Acroma, taking a wide sweep south of Tobruk by Bir Gobi and Knightsbridge, Royals and 4 S.A. Armoured Car Regiment being now under their command. Patrols of 11 Hussars had already reached Gambut and 22 Armoured Brigade advanced again at midday moving south of the Trigh Capuzzo along the old " M " route. The Queens Brigade who had only just reached Sidi Azeiz, after a long weary desert drive, cheerfully started off again as soon as they had had a meal. By last light patrols of 11 Hussars were in contact with the enemy on the perimeter of Tobruk and 4 Light Armoured Brigade had reached Knightsbridge. 22 Armoured Brigade and Divisional H.Q., followed by the Queens Brigade, leaguered just east of Sidi Rezegh. The enemy left Tobruk during the night, and on the morning of 14 November, 11 Hussars entered Tobruk while 4 Light Armoured Brigade reached Acroma. The Queens Brigade followed 11 Hussars into Tobruk and occupied the town. 22 Armoured Brigade, its tanks greatly reduced in numbers and at their last mechanical gasp, remained concentrated between El Adem and Knightsbridge. 4 Light Armoured Brigade continued the pursuit to Gazala and on to Tmimi, where an enemy rearguard was defending the aerodrome. 12 Lancers from 1 Armoured Division were brought forward and directed on Martuba, while 4 Light Armoured Brigade continued the pursuit in the broken country astride the coast road. By 16 November they had reached Derna and Martuba and pushed the enemy back to Giovanni Berta.

The tanks of 22 Armoured Brigade could go no further and administrative reasons forbade the maintenance of any large force further west, until the port of Tobruk was working. We were also in danger of outrunning our air support, although the speed at which the R.A.F. advanced and occupied new landing grounds was not the least of the remarkable feats of " Mary's Boys." We had hardly reached El Adem before fighters were swarming on its vast aerodrome. 22 Armoured Brigade were therefore left at El Adem and the Queens Brigade in Tobruk. 4 Light Armoured Brigade with 4 S.A. Armoured Car Regiment, a composite Regiment of two Squadrons of tanks from the Royal Scots Greys and 4-8 Hussars, 3 Regiment R.H.A. less one Battery and 1 Battalion K.R.R.C. less one Company, continued the difficult pursuit along the main road through the hills.

On 16 November, 11 Hussars, reinforced with a Battery from 3 Regiment R.H.A., a Company of 1 Battalion K.R.R.C. and some light A.A. Artillery, and with sufficient supplies to reach Benghasi, set off south of Bir Hacheim directed on Msus, closely followed by Main Divisional H.Q. The Royals followed with one Battery of 4 Field Regiment and a Company of 1 Battalion R.B. similarly organized, joining Divisional H.Q. about 20 miles west of Bir Hacheim on the evening of 16 November.

By the evening of 17 November, 11 Hussars reached Msus, while Divisional H.Q. and the Royals were just west of Wadi Mra, south of Bir Tengeder. On 18 November, 11 Hussars encountered enemy rearguards on the line of the escarpment between Sceleidima and Antelat. They were much hindered by heavy rain and by the activities of ME-109's which bombed and strafed unopposed. 4 Light Armoured Brigade had by this time reached Slonta and Beda Littoria, unable to get off the roads, on which mines and demolitions caused further difficulties. By the evening of 18 November, Royals and Divisional H.Q. had also reached Msus. On 19 November, 11 Hussars got down the escarpment at Antelat and Sceleidima, and in spite of difficulties caused by wet ground, were in observation of Soluch and Magrun. Royals were directed on Agedabia, but their guns got stuck and they were held up by wet ground everywhere. The Landing Ground at Msus had been cleared by a Company of 1 Battalion K.R.R.C. and 19 Lockheeds landed during the day with ammunition and petrol, taking back with them the sick and wounded.

On 20 November, 4 Light Armoured Brigade entered Benghasi from the north, 11 Hussars following close in from the south. Royals regained contact with the main enemy rearguard position north-east of Agedabia.

That evening 1 Battalion R.T.R., made up to one Light Squadron and one Heavy Squadron from all the fit tanks of the 22 Armoured Brigade and some they took over from 10 Hussars, with the remainder of 4 Field Regiment and 1 Battalion R.B. arrived at Msus, having come straight across the desert from El Adem on transporters. 22 Armoured Brigade had brought a Tactical H.Q. forward as well.

By the evening of 21 November the Light Squadron was in observation of the enemy from the ridge overlooking the village from the south-east, while the remainder of the group got about half-way between Antelat and Agedabia before leaguering. On 22 November the advance continued against Agedabia itself. North-east of the village the enemy's position extended for some five miles into the sand dunes. To the south it ran parallel to the main road. The tanks tried to outflank the position on both sides while the guns took on enemy guns near the village itself. Considerable trouble was experienced both with mines and with the soft going, and we had not been able to cut the enemy off by last light. The enemy withdrew during the night, leaving behind several guns and vehicles damaged or destroyed and some men who either had not been told or could not get the transport to get away. The advance continued along the main road, mines and sandy going being the chief causes of delay, and by 25 November we had come up against the firmest opposition we had encountered for some time just east of Mersa Brega. Further advance was clearly not possible until more troops were brought forward and the Division settled down to reconnoitring, harassing and observing the enemy.

During this period some reorganization took place. 4 Light Armoured Brigade took over the left flank, 1 Battalion K.R.R.C. being relieved by 2 Battalion K.R.R.C. and 2 Derby Yeomanry by King's Dragoon Guards. Royals remained with the Brigade. 4-8 Hussars were withdrawn to the Delta.

Brigadier M. G. Roddick had been wounded near Slonta and had been succeeded by Brigadier C. B. Harvey, who had been second-in-command of 2 Armoured Brigade, before which he had commanded 10 Hussars. 8 Armoured Brigade, consisting of 5 Regiment R.H.A., 3 Battalion R.T.R., Notts Yeomanry (Sherwood Rangers), Staffs Yeomanry, 1 Battalion Buffs and commanded by Brigadier N. Custance, relieved 22 Armoured Brigade, who settled down to re-equip at Mrassas between Tobruk and Bardia. The Queens Brigade had moved forward from Tobruk to Benghasi and later rejoined the Division near Mersa Brega. 30 Corps now took over control from 10 Corps and 2 N.Z. Division and 51 (Highland) Division were brought forward to deal with the Mersa Brega position.

On 12 December the advance was resumed. The enemy withdrew during the night and the Highland Division entered Mersa Brega the following day, while we advanced from Suera. On 14 December, 8 Armoured Brigade continued the advance and by last light were engaging the enemy's main position south-west of Agheila. The Highland Division were delayed by large numbers of mines astride the coast road and had not regained contact with the enemy east of Agheila. During 15 December, 8 Armoured Brigade engaged the enemy's main position, but they were much hampered by sand and salt marsh. The enemy withdrew again during the night and the Division followed up along the coast road, gaining contact with 2 N.Z. Division and 4 Light Armoured Brigade near Marble Arch. They had carried out a wide outflanking movement to the south of us, but had found the ground overlooking the road between Marble Arch and Nofilia impassable. The enemy, moving fast in small columns, including tanks, managed to escape the net closing round them. By last light we had secured the landing grounds at Marble Arch and Merduma, which were heavily mined, and our patrols reported signs of a stand by the enemy at Nofilia.

On 17 December the pursuit continued, 8 Armoured Brigade advancing on Nofilia from the east, while 2 N.Z. Division came at it from the south. The enemy clearly stayed longer than he meant to and lost a considerable number of tanks and guns before getting the rest of his rearguard away along the coast road towards Sirte. By 24 December we had closed up to his rearguard position just east of Sirte, which was evacuated on the night of Christmas Eve. A thick ground mist and the presence of many mines and booby traps around Sirte delayed the pursuit, and it was not until Boxing Day that we regained contact with a rearguard position of some strength on the Wadi Chebir. This rearguard withdrew on the night 27-28 December into the enemy's main position, which was found to run from the sea just north of Buerat El Hsun, southwest across the main road west of the village, thence parallel to and south of the road to about 5 miles south east of Gheddahia, whence patrols operated southwards along the line of the track to Bu Ngem. For administrative reasons 8 Armoured Brigade had not been brought forward of the area south of Sirte and contact with the enemy was maintained by 4 Light Armoured Brigade.

A pause followed while more troops were brought forward, forward Landing Grounds were made and preparations for an attack on the Buerat position began. 2 N.Z. Division had stayed behind near Nofilia and the Highland Division were still at Agheila. 8 Armoured Brigade remained in the Division, 22 Armoured Brigade being re-equipped and brought forward in Army Reserve. The Queens Brigade remained concentrated at the northern end of the Wadi Tamet. During this period the enemy developed his position, gradually extending southwards from Gheddahia. The final concentration was left as late as possible for reasons of secrecy. 51 (Highland) Division were to close up on the coast, while 2 N.Z. Division were to move parallel and to the south of us with 4 Light Armoured Brigade to the south of them. The construction of the landing grounds and the formation of the F.M.C., as well as the gradual increase in troops in the forward area, caused the enemy to send all his immobile troops back to Homs and Tarhuna. Mixed German and Italian formations held the line from the sea to south east of Gheddahia. 21 Panzer Division was believed to be near Gheddahia with 15 Panzer Division and Reconnaissance units south of it, just west of the Bu Ngem road. The country in front of us was very inadequately mapped and was intersected by many wadis. Several of these were very soft as were most parts of the Wadis Chebitr and Tamet, which complicated the business of concentration. Invaluable information of the going behind the enemy was obtained from patrols of the S.A.S. and Long Range Desert Group, who were operating at this time all over the area we were to cover. The general plan was for the Highland Division with 23 Armoured Brigade to clear the coast road, while we and 2 N.Z. Division went round the enemy's right flank, first towards Sedada and thence either straight for Tarhuna or cutting in behind the enemy if he did not withdraw. Owing to the difficulties of the ground it was impossible to cross the Bu Ngem road so far south as to avoid the enemy altogether. The concentration was therefore designed to lead the enemy to think that the main attack would be near the coast road. 154 Brigade came up ahead of the Highland Division and came under command until the 13 January, on which date 8 Armoured Brigade began to move forward.

By daylight on 14 January the whole Division was concentrated north of the Wadi Chebir and 2 N.Z. Division had come up on our left. 22 Armoured Brigade with 12 Lancers were on our right in Army Reserve. A night march along a marked and lighted route brought the head of 8 Armoured Brigade on to the Bu Ngem road at midnight, with the Queens Brigade to the north east of them. 4 Light Armoured Brigade, less Royals, who were observing the front to the left of 11 Hussars and in the front and to the left of 2 N.Z. Division, was concentrated behind 8 Armoured Brigade. At first light 8 Armoured Brigade crossed the road and soon came up against enemy tanks and anti-tank guns on the ridge to the west of it. The enemy had recently received several of the new 75 mm. anti-tank guns which were well sighted in defiladed positions behind the ridge, where Observation Posts could get no observation of them. Queens Brigade took up a position astride the Bu Ngem road north of 8 Armoured Brigade, where they were under accurate fire from the enemy positions south of Gheddahia. It was impossible to outflank the position as 2 N.Z. Division were close in on our left and restricted by soft going. By mid-day it was clear that 4 Light Armoured Brigade were not going to be able to pass through 8 Armoured Brigade ; they were therefore sent south of 2 N.Z. Division to follow the Royals, who had made some progress.

In the battle which took place that afternoon for the possession of the ridge, the enemy lost several guns and a few tanks, while we had several tanks knocked out by anti-tank guns. During the night the enemy withdrew and by 10.00 hours 11 Hussars had reported the Wadi Zem Zem clear of enemy, had found a way across without difficulty and proved the minefield dummy. 8 Armoured Brigade followed 11 Hussars, and the Queens Brigade followed them. Enemy patrols were met beyond the Zem Zem, but no rearguard position was encountered until the usual screen of anti-tank guns supported by tanks was found east of Sedada in the afternoon. These were engaged till last light and several guns destroyed. The enemy withdrew during the night, destroying the bridge over the Wadi east of Sedada.

Some delay was caused on the morning of 17 January by the difficulty of finding a route down the escarpment and across the broad sandy wadi beyond. 8 Armoured Brigade did not move on again until 12.00 hours. After negotiating the escarpment and the wadi however, a stretch of very good going was found and the Division moved very fast, crossing the Beni Ulid-Bir Dufan track north of Beni Ulid before last light. The enemy had apparently withdrawn to Beni Ulid where the Air Force reported a mass of vehicles. 4 Light Armoured Brigade had meanwhile been struggling through a defile over very bad going directed on Beni Ulid from the south. The going improved after mid-day and in the late afternoon contact was made with the enemy east of the village. The enemy vehicles were closely packed and 2 Battalion K.R.R.C. and 3 Regiment R.H.A. caused much damage, continuing to fire into the enemy transport with 6 pounders in the dark. The advance was continued north of Beni Ulid the following day 18 January. The going, however, was extremely bad, being very stony and intersected by large wadis. The greatest difficulty was encountered in finding a route down into the bed of the Wadi Tsmama. One very bad one was found, after which progress was comparatively easy. This defile, which could only be negotiated at walking pace, caused great delay. 4 Light Armoured Brigade were unable to get beyond Beni Ulid owing to demolitions. They found 13 M-13 tanks abandoned in the village. By last light Crusaders of Staffs Yeomanry were in action against vehicles and guns moving north on the road from Beni Ulid some ten miles south of Tarhuna, and patrols of 11 Hussars were in contact with the enemy about 6 miles south of the village. Owing to the bad going and the defile, the rest of the Division was very much strung out behind, most of it still east of Wadi Tmasma. It was the worst going the Division had ever encountered, worse even than the stony stretch south west of Mechili.

On 19 January 8 Armoured Brigade closed up to the enemy screen covering Tarhuna, while the rest of the Division closed up behind. The enemy's guns were concealed west of the village and he had all the observation. Few tanks were seen, though we had reason to believe that all that was left of his tanks were in the area. We were ordered not to run headlong into trouble, but to wait for 2 N.Z. Division if an attack was necessary. It was on this morning, while standing on Brigadier Custance's tank observing the enemy, that General Harding was wounded by a 75 mm. shell which landed beside the tank. He was badly wounded in the left arm and leg and also shaken by the fall off the top of the Grant Tank. It was a bitter disappointment to him, who had had Tripoli as his goal for so long, to fall out of the race when we were within a few days of the finish. The Division lost an outstanding Commander, whom every man liked, admired and respected. He had brought the Division all the way from El Alamein and the speed and the success of our advance were largely due to his foresight, determination and energy. Brigadier Custance took over temporary command for 24 hours until the arrival of Brigadier Roberts, Commander 22 Armoured Brigade. During the rest of the day little progress was made. It was found impossible to outflank the position and considerable difficulty was experienced with soft sand, of which there were several drifts. 4 Light Armoured Brigade meanwhile were struggling northwards through atrocious country west of the Beni Ulid-Tarhuna road, in face of repeated Stuka attacks. The R.A.F. bombed the road west of Tarhuna that night and on 20 January it was found that the enemy had withdrawn into the pass, through which the road to Tripoli descended into the plain of the Gefara. The enemy had every advantage of concealment and observation, and progress was difficult. 4 Light Armoured Brigade meanwhile had struggled on and began to emerge on to the track from Tarhuna to Garian, the forward patrols of K.D.G. discovering a route down into the plain below. Brigadier Roberts asked Corps if we could send an Armoured Regiment down that way in order to outflank the pass. This was not allowed as 2 N.Z. Division were to use that route. They did not, however, have more than a few patrols of N.Z. Division Cavalry in that area on that day.

No progress was made on the day of 21 January except that 4 Light Armoured Brigade got down on to the coastal plain less the Royals, supported by a Battery of 3 Regiment R.H.A., who went along the track towards Garian, east of which they were held up by mines and anti-tank guns. Preparations had been made for an attack that night, the Queens Brigade going on foot along the ridge west of the road and cutting the foot of the pass, while 8 Armoured Brigade with 1 Battalion Buffs, 3 Battalion R.T.R. and the Divisional R.E. went straight down the road. This attack coincided with the enemy's withdrawal. Large craters caused much delay, but a big bulldozer manned by South African Engineers did magnificent work, and by first light on 21 January, 3 Battalion R.T.R. were at the foot of the pass. The going in the plain below was very soft and tufty. 4 Light Armoured Brigade, directed towards Azizia, found great difficulty in moving and were confronted by 30 German tanks, which luckily did not venture far from Azizia. The leading troops of 2 N.Z. Division, including the Greys, were beginning to get down into the plain at this time, but were not near enough to 4 Light Armoured Brigade to support them. Further delay was caused by demolitions and by congestion caused in the pass by the throng of hangers-on who appeared like vultures, all intent on being first into Tripoli, provided that someone else did the fighting which they did their best to obstruct.

By midday the main enemy rearguard had been met south of Castel Benito, while 2 N.Z. Division were engaging another enemy force at Azizia. The country was fairly enclosed ; there was an anti-tank ditch to cross and the ground on either side of the road was very soft. It looked unlikely that 8 Armoured Brigade would be able to dislodge the enemy. The Queens Brigade, who had been left in the pass at the opposite end from their transport, were ordered at 14.00 hours to move up and prepare to attack Castel Benito after dark. This move was a model of speed in embussing and movement. All other traffic was moved off the road on to one side, which was not easy, being nose to tail all the way along, and by 17.30 hours the Brigade was complete in its assembly area. They attacked that night, but the enemy, who had nearly been cut off by 3 Battalion R.T.R., withdrew westwards and Castel Benito was found unoccupied.

At first light, or slightly before, on 23 January, 11 Hussars complete, followed by Tactical Divisional Headquarters, drove into Tripoli unopposed, beating the tanks of 23 Armoured Brigade with the Highland Division by about 4 hours—3 months to a day after the opening of the battle of El Alamein.

Chapter VI

TRIPOLI TO TUNIS

January to May 1943

THE immediate result of the capture of Tripoli was an outbreak of Tripoli fever   in other words more attention was paid to Tripoli than to the enemy. We were lucky enough to recover from it about midday on 23 January. Others continued to suffer from it for several weeks. At about midday 11 Hussars began to move west along the coast road and regained contact with enemy patrols covering the anti-tank ditch west of Zanzur. 8 Armoured Brigade moved from Castel Benito to Zanzur and prepared to dislodge the enemy. The Queens Brigade moved to Suani Ben Adem on the Azizia Road. There were still enemy in the area of Bianchi, and King's Dragoon Guards patrols of 4 Light Armoured Brigade had met an enemy rearguard west of Bianchi on the road running south from Zauia. The Royals had succeeded in entering Garian, where they were hailed by the Italians as protectors against the Arabs. They met at Garian the force of Fighting French under General Leclerc, which had come all the way from Lake Chad. They had come to the end of their petrol and it was not possible to supply them, as the pass up the escarpment to Garian had been well and truly blown.

At this time Major-General G. W. E. J. Erskine was appointed to command the Division. He was well known to the Division, having been BGS of 13 Corps from the time that General Gott assumed command of it in April, 1942, until he became temporarily BGS of Eighth Army in December. He came out to the Middle East as Commander of 69 Brigade in 50 Division, before which he had commanded 2 Battalion K.R.R.C. He was, therefore, the third "Greenjacket" to command the Division. At the same time Brigadier Roberts left, originally to go home. From this, however, he was diverted to command 26 Armoured Brigade of 6 Armoured Division in Tunisia. The Division owed much to Brigadier Roberts. At the outbreak of war he was Adjutant of 6 Battalion R.T.R. He then became DAQMG of the Division, went to the Staff College at Haifa and returned as Brigade Major to 4 Armoured Brigade in the winter of 1940-41. He then became GSO II of the Division which he left in September, 1941, to become AQMG of 30 Corps. He took over command of 3 Battalion R.T.R., then in 4 Armoured Brigade, in February, 1942, was wounded in May when his tank caught fire, returned to command again and was appointed to command 22 Armoured Brigade in July. He had a difficult task as every Regiment was then mixed with bits of at least one other Regiment and few of them had fought together before. He welded 22 Armoured Brigade into a most formidable formation. His outstanding leadership and almost uncanny skill won him the affection, admiration and confidence of every man in his Brigade. He was succeeded by Brigadier W. R. N. Hinde, who had commanded an Armoured Brigade in England after commanding 15-19 Hussars. At the same time Brigadier C. B. Harvey took over command of 8 Armoured Brigade, Brigadier D. S. Newton-King taking over command of 4 Light Armoured Brigade. He was then Second-in-command of 22 Armoured Brigade and had been well known to all as the original Commanding Officer of 4 S.A. Armoured Car Regiment.

By 25 January the enemy had been forced back to Zauia on the coast and 4 Light Armoured Brigade had entered Iefren in the south. The pass here was blown, but not as badly as at Garian and 4 Field Squadron were able to repair it. Between the narrow fertile strip, a mile or two wide, along which the coast road ran, and the foot of the escarpment in the south, there is a wide expanse of sand dunes passable to no vehicles except jeeps and light tracked vehicles. Both Crusaders and Shermans got into difficulties in these dunes. It was not possible, therefore, to outflank the enemy by any local move. The administrative situation, particularly petrol supply, was also difficult at this time. Divisional R.A.S.C. were still re-filling at the F.M.C. 25 miles north-east of Beni Ulid and further difficulties were caused by the delayed action demolitions in Tarhuna pass. For both tactical and administrative reasons it was decided therefore to continue the advance along the coast with the Queens Brigade, supported by the remaining Valentines of 40 Battalion R.T.R., 5 Regiment R.H.A. and 69 Medium Regiment. 12 Lancers relieved 11 Hussars, whose Armoured Cars were fast wearing out. The Queens Brigade relieved 8 Armoured Brigade at Zauia, Notts Yeomanry remaining in Zauia area and the rest of the Brigade returning to Zanzur. The advance from Zanzur to Zuaia, which was captured on 31 January, was not an easy one. Observation was hindered by palm trees, going off the road was difficult for wheeled vehicles and all roads and tracks were thick with mines and booby traps. Every bridge and culvert was blown. Great credit is due to all the men of the Queens who fought all the way on their feet, to the engineers who dealt with the mines and demolitions under fire, working all day and night—they had a particularly difficult task in the salt marshes east of Zuaia—to the 40 Battalion R.T.R., who kept their ancient and worn out Valentines going only by almost superhuman efforts, and cheerfully went into action, knowing their chances of breaking down were 10 to 1 on ; to the Gunners who by speed and accuracy ensured that, if the enemy stood, he paid for it ; to the 12 Lancers who showed their determination to get on by resorting to camels, ponies and donkeys or to their feet, when their armoured cars could not get on. Meanwhile the 4 Light Armoured Brigade, extended to the utmost limit, were working along the escarpment to the south and were the first to cross the frontier into Tunisia, which they did on 2 February. The enemy tried to hang on to Zuara, but the Valentines, carrying some of the Queens on the tanks, and one Squadron of the 12 Lancers managed to struggle through the sand dunes south of the salt marshes east of Zuara and force the enemy to withdraw again. The Queens Brigade pushed on over very difficult country, meeting more mines every day, until they reached Pisida. 12 Lancers patrols reached El Assa on the 2 February and were in contact with enemy patrols on the line of the salt marsh running along the frontier. South of them 4 Light Armoured Brigade were in contact with their old enemies 3 and 33 Reconnaissance Units west of the frontier. The Queens Brigade were faced by a bare open spit of land, only 500 yards wide at its narrowest point, between the sea and the salt marsh. South of the main salt marsh was a stretch of sand dunes and south of that cultivated land round El Assa, intersected by salt marsh.

The salt marsh which ran down the frontier was at its narrowest some 15 miles north-west of El Assa ; south of that again no crossing could be found except by a long detour through El Uotia. The narrow crossing was held by the enemy and was only passable in dry weather. The Division was now very extended, while the enemy, by holding the few crossings, could concentrate a superior force including at least 30 tanks against us. 8 Armoured Brigade had about 40 fit tanks left : these were all given to Staffs Yeomanry and the Brigade brought forward, less 3 Battalion R.T.R. and Notts Yeomanry. 146 Field Regiment, less one Battery, which remained with 4 Light Armoured Brigade, relieved 5 Regiment R.H.A. with the Queens Brigade. Owing to shortage of transport and equipment, 3 Regiment R.H.A., Royals and two Companies of 2 Battalion K.R.R.C. had to be left out of battle. 11 Hussars were re-equipping on a new establishment for more enclosed country. Between the 4 and 8 February, preparations were made for the advance across the frontier to Ben Gardane. 8 Armoured Brigade moved forward to the area of Zuara, and on 7 February advanced to El Assa. On the night 7-8 February the Brigade moved north, and on the morning of 8 February drove in the enemy rearguard covering the crossing and began to move across.

The enemy we feared most then began to attack us—rain. The 200 yards of salt marsh soon became impassable to wheels, but enough were got over to form a bridgehead on the far side. The Engineers laboured to make a temporary crossing with stones from the houses of El Assa, but the approaches deteriorated and the crossing itself continually broke through. By towing with tanks and half-tracks on six-wheeled vehicles, 5 Regiment R.H.A., 1 Battalion Buffs and 12 Lancers got their vehicles across. The rain continued unabated. It was clear that such a makeshift crossing could not take the rest of the Division. Traffic was therefore limited to the maintenance of the bridgehead, while the Divisional R.E. collected wood and nails from all over Tripolitania to build a wooden causeway capable of taking everything except tanks. It was estimated that it would take until 12.00 hours 14 February to complete. Meanwhile 153 Brigade of 51 (Highland) Division relieved the Queens Brigade at Pisida and the latter moved to El Assa. 22 Armoured Brigade, in Corps Reserve, moved to El Uotia, ready to advance in conformity with us. 4 Light Armoured Brigade worked gradually forward until they had almost closed in on Foum Tatahouine and had secured the vital pass up into the southern plateau south of it. They were restricted by the bad going to movement on tracks and roads and were having a particularly unpleasant time from the enemy's Air Force. The R.A.F. moved up to the landing ground at El Assa, where they had only a salt marsh between them and the enemy's Reconnaissance Units. The Causeway, as it was called, was ready two hours before time on the 14 February. The remainder of 8 Armoured Brigade and 69 Medium Regiment crossed that day, the Queens

Brigade going over during the night. By 09.00 hours 15 February, the whole Division was across. 8 Armoured Brigade and the Queens Brigade advanced towards Ben Gardane side by side, 50 Battalion R.T.R. supporting the Queens. The enemy withdrew rapidly and 153 Brigade began to advance along the coast road, where they had much trouble with mines of all kinds.

The Queens Brigade went straight for Ben Gardane, while 8 Armoured Brigade cut across to the main road west of it. The going everywhere was very slow, being soft sand. By last light the whole of Ben Gardane area was occupied, and contact was established with the main enemy rearguard position on the line of a broad shallow wadi about 10 miles west of the town. The enemy withdrew all except a light mobile rearguard during the night. 8 Armoured Brigade continued the advance south of the main road during 16 February, but progress was very slow on account of the very bad going. 12 Lancers and the Queens Brigade advanced along the line of the road and the track north of it, their progress depending mainly on the rate of progress of the Engineers clearing mines. By last light both the Queens Brigade and the 8 Armoured Brigade had reached Nefatia. The 8 Armoured Brigade now had only 12 fit tanks left. 22 Armoured Brigade had moved up to Ben Gardane and on 17 February relieved 8 Armoured Brigade, 5 Regiment R.H.A. coming under command of 22 Armoured Brigade. The Queens Brigade remained at Nefatia, while the 12 Lancers pushed their patrols up to the edge of Medenine and the Divisional R.E. repaired craters on the road practically up to Medenine itself. Reconnaissance near Medenine was limited by a thick mist, which never lifted and reduced visibility to less than a mile. Invaluable reconnaissance was, however, done of the wadis north of the main road and crossings were found. The enemy were holding Metameur and the hills known as the Tadjeras, which dominated the whole area. On the night 18-19 February, 22 Armoured Brigade advanced along the road to Point 118, about three miles east of Medenine, followed by the Divisional Artillery and the Queens Brigade. The usual mist covered the area on the morning of 19 February. Under cover of this mist 22 Armoured Brigade, with 5 Battalion R.T.R. leading, crossed the wadi north of the road and made straight across country to cut the road to Mareth north of the Tadjeras. They moved fast and succeeded in reaching the hill, later known as 5th Tanks Hill, which overlooked the road, before 10.00 hours, just as the mist began to lift. 4 County of London Yeomanry came up on their right and 1 Battalion R.T.R. on the left, 5 Regiment R.H.A. coming into action to the east of them. When the mist lifted they found themselves completely overlooked by the Tadjeras and came under accurate shell fire. There was, however, some cover in the ground and the Brigade was in position before the enemy realised they were there. Several vehicles trying to get away up the road were destroyed and some prisoners captured. Some trouble was encountered with mines near the road. The rest of the day was spent in closing in on the enemy and engaging his guns, while the Queens Brigade with 50 Battalion R.T.R. entered Medenine, and closed up to the position east of Metameur as fast as the work of the R.Es. in clearing mines and repairing craters allowed. The whole area between Medenine and Metameur was thick with anti-personnel and anti-tank mines. 1 Battalion R.B. blocked the road near Bir Koutine that night and the enemy withdrew north-west into the hills just east of the Mareth Line. The Division occupied the Tadjeras on the evening of 20 February. We knew that the enemy did not mean to give up this ground easily. Its capture by us was essential before any approach to the Mareth Line could take place. We won it by surprise due not a little to the mist. Credit goes to the 12 Lancers for their previous reconnaissance and to 22 Armoured Brigade for the speed with which they advanced to cut the road and the determination with which they held on and improved their gains, once the surprise was lost and the mist lifted. In the next few days we improved our position, the Queens Brigade securing the Tadjeras and 12 Lancers extending their reconnaissance up to the line of the wadi Zessar. 22 Armoured Brigade remained in position north-west of the Tadjeras. 4 Light Armoured Brigade meanwhile had surrounded Foum Tatahouine, in the face of great difficulties caused by the vast front they covered, the formidable nature of the country, their shortage of transport and the slenderness of their resources. In spite of all this they captured Foum Tatahouine by a brilliant action by one Company of 2 Battalion K.R.R.C. and opened up the road thence to Medenine, the enemy withdrawing into the mountains west of the road. 201 Guards Brigade, who had been reformed in Syria since the original Brigade had been lost in Tobruk, now arrived having travelled all the way by road, and relieved the Queens Brigade on the Tadjeras. The Queens Brigade, by a night attack, occupied the high ground west of the Tadjeras, known as Abdalla and Point 214. This gave us a naturally strong position extending south of the Wadi Zessar, across which 12 Lancers had now got a patrol in the area later known as Fort George. 4 Light Armoured Brigade continued to probe into the mountains, forcing the enemy further north and establishing contact with General Leclerc's Fighting French, who had come up on the far side of the mountains.

The Highland Division followed close on our heels and took over the front from the coast down to the main road. One big problem for some time and one of the reasons why the Medenine area was essential to us was the lack of suitable areas for landing grounds. Medenine was the first area west of Tripolitania where such ground existed. Unfortunately, soon after the R.A.F. had begun to use the landing grounds they made south of Medenine, the enemy brought a 170 mm. gun into the edge of the hills south-west of Medenine and shelled the western landing ground, making it unusable. During this period the 1 Battalion Buffs came ahead of 8 Armoured Brigade and took over a wide front covering Medenine from the west. The positions we occupied at this time were all under observation by the enemy and movement, especially in the Queens' area, invariably drew accurate shellfire. 4 Light Armoured Brigade was reinforced by the First Fighting French Flying column and Brigadier J. C. Currie, who had been commanding 9 Armoured Brigade, and whose vigorous personality was well known to the Division from the days when he had succeeded Jock Campbell in command of 4 Regiment R.H.A. It became clear that the enemy was planning some counter-move at the beginning of March. 2 N.Z. Division came up and took over the front south of Metameur and 8 Armoured Brigade, re-equipped with tanks from the 2 Armoured Brigade, came up from Bir Gardane, coming under our command and remaining in reserve behind the centre of the front. 22 Armoured Brigade was still in the area north and north-west of the Tadjeras with battle positions reconnoitred to support different sectors of the front. On the evening of 5 March an attack by Germans and Italians was made on the northern sector of the Highland Division outpost line on the Wadi Zeuss.

This got as far as the west bank of the Wadi Zessar, but no attempt was made to attack the main position on the east bank. On the morning of 6 March, patrols of A Squadron 12 Lancers met enemy tanks on the Toujane road about 6 miles west of Metameur. It soon became apparent that the enemy had concentrated most, if not all, of his tanks in this area and was making for the Tadjeras. At the same time the enemy advanced down the main road from Mareth, but did not push this attack home. His tanks moved east until they met the dummy minefield in front of 3 Coldstream Guards, north-west of Metameur ; they turned north and ran right on to the anti-tank guns of the 2 Scots Guards, who knocked out 12. This diverted the attack still further north against the 1-6 and 1-7 Queens. The enemy pressed home his attack in spite of heavy and concentrated artillery fire, and anxious moments were caused when a few tanks got into the wadi between the 1-6 Queens and 2 Scots Guards. These, however, were dealt with by the light squadron of 1 Battalion R.T.R., which had moved over in support. The enemy stood off for a bit and tried again against the Queens' late in the morning. The Queens stood their ground and, with the help of the 65 Anti-Tank Regiment and two troops of Shermans from 1 Battalion R.T.R., knocked out all tanks which reached or penetrated their positions and made the rest withdraw. At least 100 enemy tanks attacked them and the Queens fought magnificently. The Divisional Artillery, reinforced by 58 Field Regiment and 7 and 69 Medium Regiments fired ceaselessly with great speed and accuracy all day. In the afternoon the enemy reorganized. By this time 8 Armoured Brigade had been moved across in readiness to support the 3 Coldstream Guards near Metameur. At about 16.00 hours the enemy attacked with tanks and infantry on this sector. They were met first by devastating fire from our Divisional Artillery, the N.Z. Divisional Artillery and the Mediums, and then by the machine guns of 3 Coldstream Guards. The attack petered out after a few tanks had reached the right of the N.Z. Division, where 28 Maori Battalion held a very wide front. During the night the enemy was heard to move into the area of his first attack, the junction between the Guards and the Queens. Heavy concentrations by all available guns, on previously registered Defensive Fire tasks which covered the area, were put down at 01.30, 02.30, and 03.30 hours. This finished him off, and he withdrew during the remaining hours of darkness back behind and into his original positions. We had repeated the bloody nose we had given him before the battle of El Alamein. He left 45 German tanks on our front and lost 7 to 2 N.Z. Division. We knew that not only our old enemies 15 and 21 Panzer Divisions, but a new enemy the 10 Panzer Division, took part in this attack and that their casualties were heavy. It was a badly conceived attack, poorly carried out. He carried out no reconnaissance and never concentrated his artillery. The battle was won by the Queens, the Guards, the 65 Anti-Tank Regiment (Norfolk Yeomanry), our own Gunners and those who supported us. A minor but vital part was played by A Squadron 12 Lancers, who gave the first warning, and by 1 Battalion R.T.R., who prevented the tanks, which had escaped the Anti-Tank guns, from getting any further. 4 Light Armoured Brigade had had their battle against a detachment in the south, in which the Flying Column did great work. The Battle of Medenine lasted only 24 hours, but it made the battle of Mareth possible and cost the enemy dear. Our own casualties were very light. After this battle until the 21 March, re-organization of the front was continually taking place, as new formations arrived or moved round. By the 16th, 201 Guards Brigade had taken over the sector immediately south of Fort George. The Queens Brigade extended their right to the left of the Guards, 1 Armoured Division taking over the Tadjeras and Point 214. As a preliminary to the main operation we had to capture Sidi Guela, a formidable strong point held by part of the 90 Light Division, which overlooked the whole area in which the Artillery to support the main attack was to be deployed and the left of which was to be protected by the Highland Division. It was not an easy undertaking. Little detailed reconnaissance of the area had been done, as a wide no-man's-land had existed between the wadis Zessar and Zeuss in this area. It entailed crossing the wadi Zeuss, which appeared possible in only a few places, one at least of which was known to be mined. The high ground was steep and the enemy had dug himself well in. The Guards Brigade took on this stiff task, attacking on the night of 16-17, supported by a very great concentration of artillery. In spite of great difficulties caused by the wadi and the thick belt of anti-personnel and anti-tank mines, 6 Grenadier Guards on the right and 3 Coldstream Guards on the left reached their objectives. After they had reached them enemy machine gun posts, which had been silenced by the artillery programme, came to life again behind and among the Guards. These caused many casualties, particularly in the area of the minefield. Both Battalions beat off several counter-attacks, but it was impossible to get Carriers, Mortars, Machine Guns and Anti-tank guns forward and by first light it was clear that the positions were untenable. Smoke was put down to allow those who could to withdraw, but one complete Company of 3 Coldstream Guards and about half of 6 Grenadiers never came back. These two Battalions suffered heavily, particularly in officer casualties. They had fought like tigers and had not fought in vain. It was not until later that we discovered how heavy the enemy's casualties had been. Not only did the Guards inflict heavy losses on the best of the German Infantry (361 Panzer Grenadier Regiment of 90 Light Division), but they tied 90 Light Division to the area of Arram and to the south of it until well after the main attack had been launched, and focussed his attention on this vital salient in his line. The Battle of Mareth proper opened on 21 March by the attack of 50 Division on the northern end of the line across the Wadi Zigzaou, the intervening ground being taken by 50 and 51 Divisions in a series of preliminary operations during the two days before. We had passed to command of 10 Corps, our task being to hold the front between Fort George and Abdalla, to be prepared to support the Highland Division in case of a counter-attack or threat to their flank, and to follow 1 Armoured Division in the event of a breakthrough. After the Germans had counter-attacked, 50 Division on the far side of the Wadi Zigzaou and the situation there became doubtful, 5 Battalion R.T.R. were sent up in support of 151 Brigade to help form a firm base on the east bank of the wadi. On the following day the Division came under command of 30 Corps again, and the whole of 22-Armoured Brigade was moved west of the Wadi Zessar north of Fort George, 4 County of London Yeomanry joining 5 Battalion R.T.R. in support of the right of the Highland Division. The presence of the tanks in that area did much to help reorganization, but they were out of range of German tanks on the far side of the wadi. It was an unpleasant spot and they came in for some heavy and accurate shelling. They were withdrawn after the front had been stabilized. 1 Armoured Division were now sent down south of Fort Tatahouine to cross the hills and join 2 N.Z. Division, while 4 Indian

Division were sent into the hills to capture Kreddache and open the road through the mountains to Bir Soltane. The Division now became responsible for holding the front down to Metameur again, as well as having the task of being prepared to support any part of the front with 22 Armoured Brigade. A lot of re-shuffling took place which ended in the Guards taking over on the left of the Queens, with 1 Battalion R.B. on their left and 4 Light Armoured Brigade on the extreme left. During the period in which 10 Corps were concentrating for the battle which ended at El Hamma, 1 Battalion R.B. and 2 Battalion K.R.R.C. carried out some very difficult local attacks against the enemy positions on the precipitous hills west of Metameur. These were carried out with great gallantry and skill, and ended in the capture of a large part of Pistoia Division. As a result of the successful battle of El Hamma, the enemy withdrew from the Mareth line just when 4 Indian Division were beginning to threaten his position in the hills by Toujane. We were told to stay where we were, but were allowed to advance if we did not use the road. A route was therefore cleared from Metameur through the Mareth Line where it met the mountains and then up a good track to El M'dou, about 10 miles south-west of Gabes ; by 30 March the whole Division was concentrated just south of El M'dou, out of contact with the enemy for the first time since we left El Alamein.

The Division had no major part to play in the battle of the Wadi Akarit which took place on 6 April. The whole of the Divisional Artillery, however, took part in the Artillery programme, and 4 County of London Yeomanry had a difficult task operating on a wide front in support of 51 (Highland) Division and 50 Division. Their role was to prevent any enemy counter-attacks with tanks from pushing the infantry off their objectives, before their anti-tank defence could be organized. This they were successful in doing, losing several tanks, however, and suffering casualties among tank commanders from sniping. The rest of 22 Armoured Brigade were moved up during 6 April, and 1 Battalion R.T.R. relieved the right squadron of 4 County of London Yeomanry in support of 51 (Highland) Division. The enemy withdrew on the night of 6-7 and the Division advanced on the left of the Highland Division, who were moving up the coast road with 23 Armoured Brigade. Owing to the delays in making gaps through the minefields and crossings over the wadi, the Division did not get more than 10 miles beyond the Akarit line by nightfall on the 7th. The country was intersected by deep soft wadis and night movement was not possible. Contact with the enemy was gained in the morning west of Skhira, where we met the much vaunted Tiger or Mark VI tank for the first time. One live Tiger, which had broken down, was captured by an enterprising patrol of 11 Hussars. 8 Armoured Brigade with 2 N.Z. Division were advancing parallel to us close on our left, and 23 Armoured Brigade with the Highland Division coming up on the coast road, where they were delayed by mines and demolitions. After being engaged by 22 Armoured Brigade, the enemy withdrew to the high ground north-west of Achichina where he was engaged by 2 N.Z. Division and ourselves up to last light, gradually being forced back all the time. The enemy withdrew again during the night and we advanced north-east, 2 N.Z. Division and the rest of 10 Corps continuing northwards. Contact with enemy patrols and a few anti-tank guns was made north of Chahal, but his resistance did not begin to stiffen until 22 Armoured Brigade and 11 Hussars reached the high ground some 6 miles south-west of Agareb at about 14.00 hours. We were fighting in conditions strange to us, the whole country being covered with olive groves and observation therefore difficult. The going was very heavy and slow for wheels. The enemy were surprised on the high ground, and, after a short action, withdrew to the ridge about 2 miles south-west of Agareb. A rearguard of field and anti-tank guns reinforced by tanks was covering the movement of a considerable amount of traffic—the whole of 15 Panzer Division—through Agareb from the west. 5 Battalion R.T.R. on the right of the road were held up by a steep-sided wadi, but 1 Battalion R.T.R. on the left of the road got well on, surprised the enemy and got right among the traffic, both the tanks and the Motor Company, C Company, 1 Battalion R.B., doing a great deal of damage. The action went on until last light, by which time the leading tanks were on the edge of the village. The enemy withdrew fast down the road towards Sfax during the night. On the morning of 10 April, 11 Hussars entered Sfax just ahead of 23 Armoured Brigade and the Highland Division, while 22 Armoured Brigade moved across country to the area 10 miles north-west of Sfax without meeting opposition. 8 Armoured Brigade under 2 N.Z. Division had meanwhile reached Triaga and continued up the road to La Hencha north of us, without meeting opposition. 11 Hussars made contact with them there and got beyond Chebba on the coast, north of which they were held up by a demolition where the road crossed a saltmarsh.

10 Corps continued the advance up to Sousse and we were told that we should not move for a fortnight. However, this was soon cancelled and the 12th saw us on the move again to join 10 Corps at Kairouan. It was a long march through Triaga and La Fauconerrie. The Queens' troop-carrying transport had been sent back to Gabes to bring up 4 Indian Division and other transport had to be collected ; but by midnight on the night 12-13 the Division was concentrated just south of Kairouan, where we met 6 Armoured Division of First Army with whom were 1 Derby Yeomanry commanded by Lt.-Col. Payne Galway, whom we had all known well when he commanded a Squadron of 11 Hussars, and 26 Armoured Brigade commanded by Brigadier Roberts. 4 Light Armoured Brigade, who had come forward with 10 Corps, came under our command again here : they were in contact with the enemy south of Djebibina between General Leclerc's Fighting French, who also came under our command, and the 19 French Corps, who were in the mountains to the west of us. On 16 April the Division moved forward again to the area of Sbikha, 22 Armoured Brigade concentrating in the plain between there and Djebel Fadeloun, held by General Leclerc. In the next few days 4 Light Armoured Brigade pushed forward to Djebibina and the Queens Brigade took over the western slopes of Djebel Fadeloun from the Fighting French, 22 Armoured Brigade supporting the left flank of the Queens and covering the gap between them and 4 Light Armoured Brigade. From 20 to 27 April the Division closed further in, pushing the enemy back to the foothills north of Djebibina and the high ground just south of Saouaf, while 4 Indian Division attacked Djebel Garci and 2 N.Z. Division attacked and captured Enfidaville and Takruna. On the 28th the Division, less 4 Light Armoured Brigade, withdrew from the area west of Djebel Fadeloun and moved round to south-west of Enfidaville, in preparation for the attack which was being planned to capture Bou Ficha and exploit to Hammamet.

By this time the First Army had attacked further north and captured Medjez el Bab and Goubellat. A sudden and unexpected change in plans followed, and the night of 30 April-1 May found the Division moving off through Maktar to Le Krib to join First Army. The tanks of 22 Armoured Brigade on transporters had to follow a much longer route through Kasserine, arriving at Le Krib on 2 May after a journey of nearly 300 miles. Here the Division came under 9 Corps General J. T. Crocker, known to many as Brigade Major to the original Tank Brigade, had been wounded shortly before and General Horrocks came over from 10 Corps to command. A few days were spent at Le Krib in reconnoitring the ground east of Medjez el Bab and getting some new tanks from First Army. On 5 May the Division advanced on two routes, one straight up the main road through Medjez el Bab, the other through El Aroussa to just south of Medjez el Bab 22 Armoured Brigade led, followed by 11 Hussars and the Queens Brigade. The Divisional Artillery, less 5 Regiment R.H.A., who were with 22 Armoured Brigade, were taking part in the artillery programme. By 07.00 hours on 6 May the leading Regiments of 22 Armoured Brigade were on the high ground which had been our Forward Defended Localities east of Medjez el Bab, immediately behind 4 Indian Division, who had reached their first objective. When 4 Indian Division had reached their second objective, the Brigade concentrated in the open ground in front of them. As soon as the artillery programme for the capture of the final objective was over, that is at 11.00 hours, the Brigade advanced to the infantry's final objective, with 26 Armoured Brigade close on their right. After 5 Battalion R.T.R. had engaged some anti-tank guns immediately to their front and 4 County of London Yeomanry had engaged a few tanks on their left, the Brigade advanced, meeting little opposition, to Massicault and the Djebel Achour, the high ground to the north of it. This was secured by 16.00 hours and patrols pushed on to the outskirts of St. Cyprien. 1-7 Queens moved up to join 22 Armoured Brigade, who leaguered for the night in that area. The advance was resumed at first light, 11 Hussars observing the left, with one Squadron under command of 22 Armoured Brigade. The rest of the Queens Brigade moved to the area of Massicault. Some opposition was met in the area of St. Cyprien and there were some 15 enemy tanks, including a tiger, on the right of the Brigade, but by midday the western slopes of the high ground north of St. Cyprien had been secured. The Queens Brigade were then ordered forward to this area and 22 Armoured Brigade advanced to capture the ridge overlooking Tunis. The enemy had several anti-tank guns, mostly 88 mm., on this ridge they were quickly dealt with and by 15.00 hours the Brigade was overlooking Tunis. There were still some enemy tanks on the right flank, which was very open as 26 Armoured Brigade were some way behind. These, however, withdrew when they and their soft vehicles were engaged from the rear by 1 Battalion R.T.R., who were astride the main road on the ridge north-east of La Mornaghia. At 15.00 hours 22 Armoured Brigade were ordered to advance into Tunis. 1 Battalion R.T.R. went straight down the road, with 5 Battalion R.T.R. on their left and 4 County of London Yeomanry on the left of them. By 16.00 hours 1 Battalion R.T.R. had reached the road junction just east of Manouba and 11 Hussars continued the chase into the city itself. The enemy were completely surprised and 11 Hussars found themselves embarrassed as much by the enthusiasm of the French population as by the mass of prisoners. Several pockets of resistance proved very troublesome. 5 Battalion R.T.R. concentrated at Le Bardo, while 4 County of London

Yeomanry watched the road to Djedeida. The Queens Brigade followed on and occupied the town, after several small engagements to mop up enemy resistance. At first light on the morning of 8 May, 22 Armoured Brigade turned north with one Squadron of 11 Hussars, while the Queens continued to round up prisoners. 5 Battalion R.T.R. moved north-east towards Carthage, capturing a large number of Luftewaffe personnel. 1 Battalion R.T.R. moved up the main road to Bizerta and regained contact with the enemy rearguard at Protville, on commanding ground covering the bridge over the river Medjerda. After a short engagement the enemy withdrew hurriedly, blowing the bridge. 1 Battalion R.T.R. occupied the high ground, but could not cross the river. However, they overlooked the road on the far side of the river and inflicted considerable damage on traffic using the road. 4 County of London Yeomanry met an enemy rearguard at Djedeida and after dealing with that, joined 1 Battalion R.T.R. on the southern bank of the river Medjerda. On the morning of 9 May American troops could be seen approaching from the west, on the far side of the valley of the Medjerda. 4 County of London Yeomanry got some Crusaders over the river and a patrol of 11 Hussars joined the Americans and actually got into Porto Farina ahead of them. Here they found a seething mass of prisoners, which included the whole of 15 Panzer Division, including its Commander.

So, for the 7 Armoured Division, ended the fighting in North Africa. It was a source of great pride and honour to have been the first to enter Tunis and it gave the Division great pleasure to do it in company with the 4 Indian Division, with whom we had begun the first real offensive in the Western Desert at the Battle of Sidi Barrani on December 8, 1940. We had travelled 2,000 miles from El Alamein, in six months almost to a day. We could feel that the task, for which we had been formed and trained and for which we had fought for so long, was well accomplished, and that those who had fallen in the dust of the desert had not fought in vain. Many of us must have wished that Strafer, Jock and the many gallant men like them, whom we should see no more, had been spared to see the day when the Seventh Armoured Division entered Tunis first of all the Troops of the United Nations in North Africa.

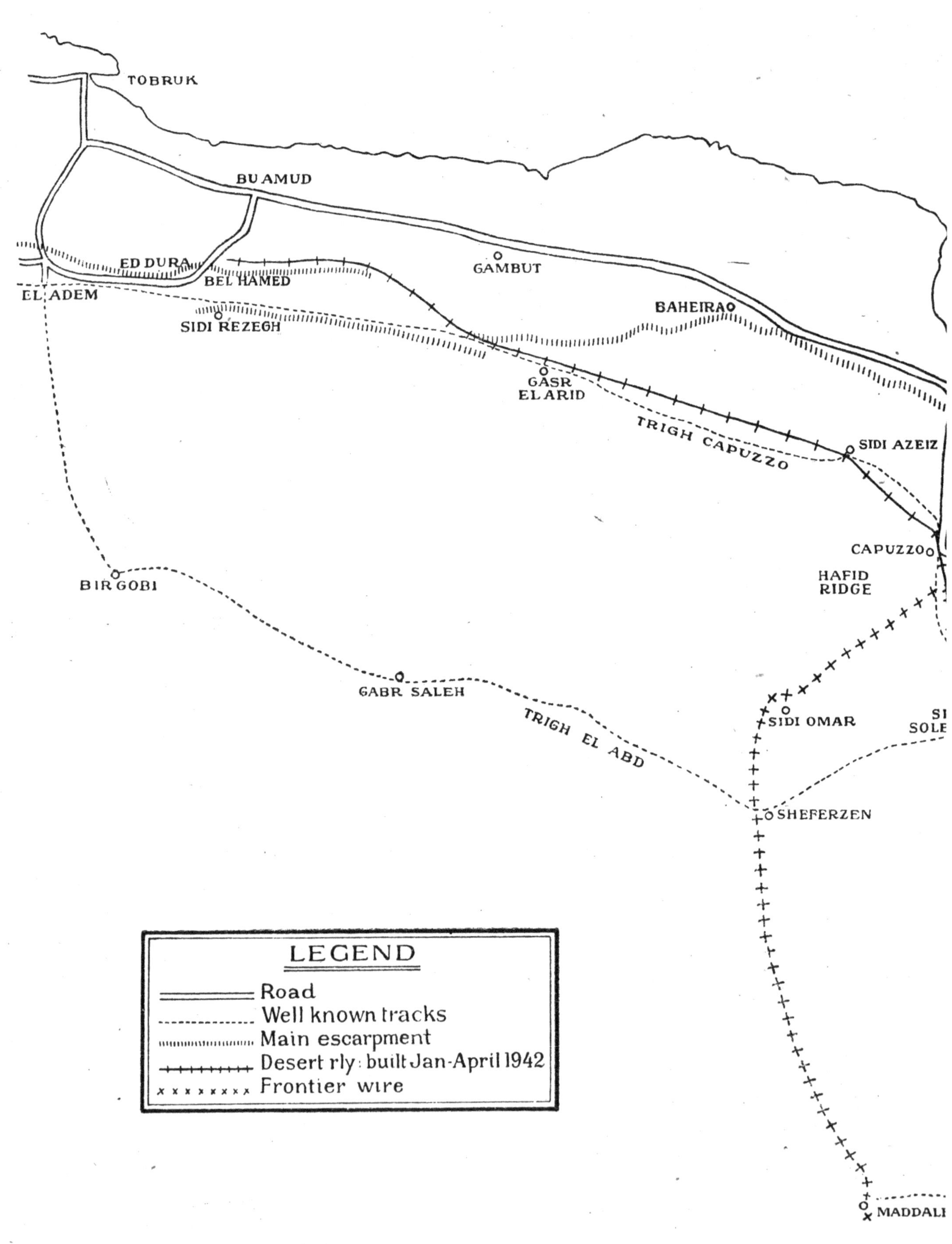
TOBRUK
BU AMUD
ED DURA
BEL HAMED
EL ADEM
GAMBUT
SIDI REZEGH
BAHEIRA
GASR
EL ARID
TRIGH CAPUZZO
SIDI AZEIZ
CAPUZZO
HAFID
RIDGE
BIR GOBI
GABR SALEH
TRIGH EL ABD
SIDI OMAR
SHEFERZEN
MADDALI
LEGEND
Road
Well known tracks
Main escarpment
Desert rly: built Jan-April 1942
Frontier wire

MAP I

THE FRONTIER
COCKPIT OF THE WESTERN DESERT

SCALE. 1/500,000

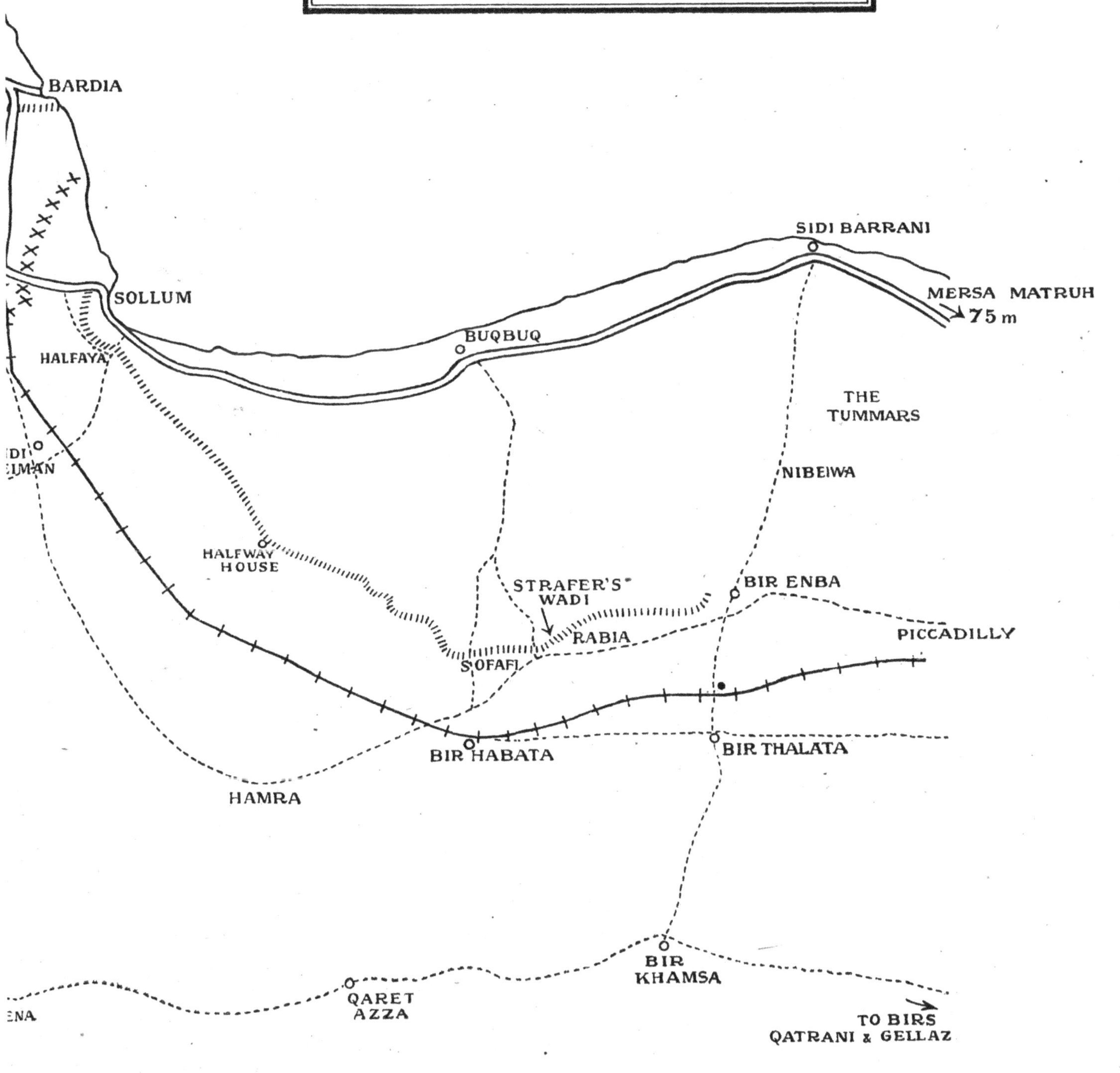

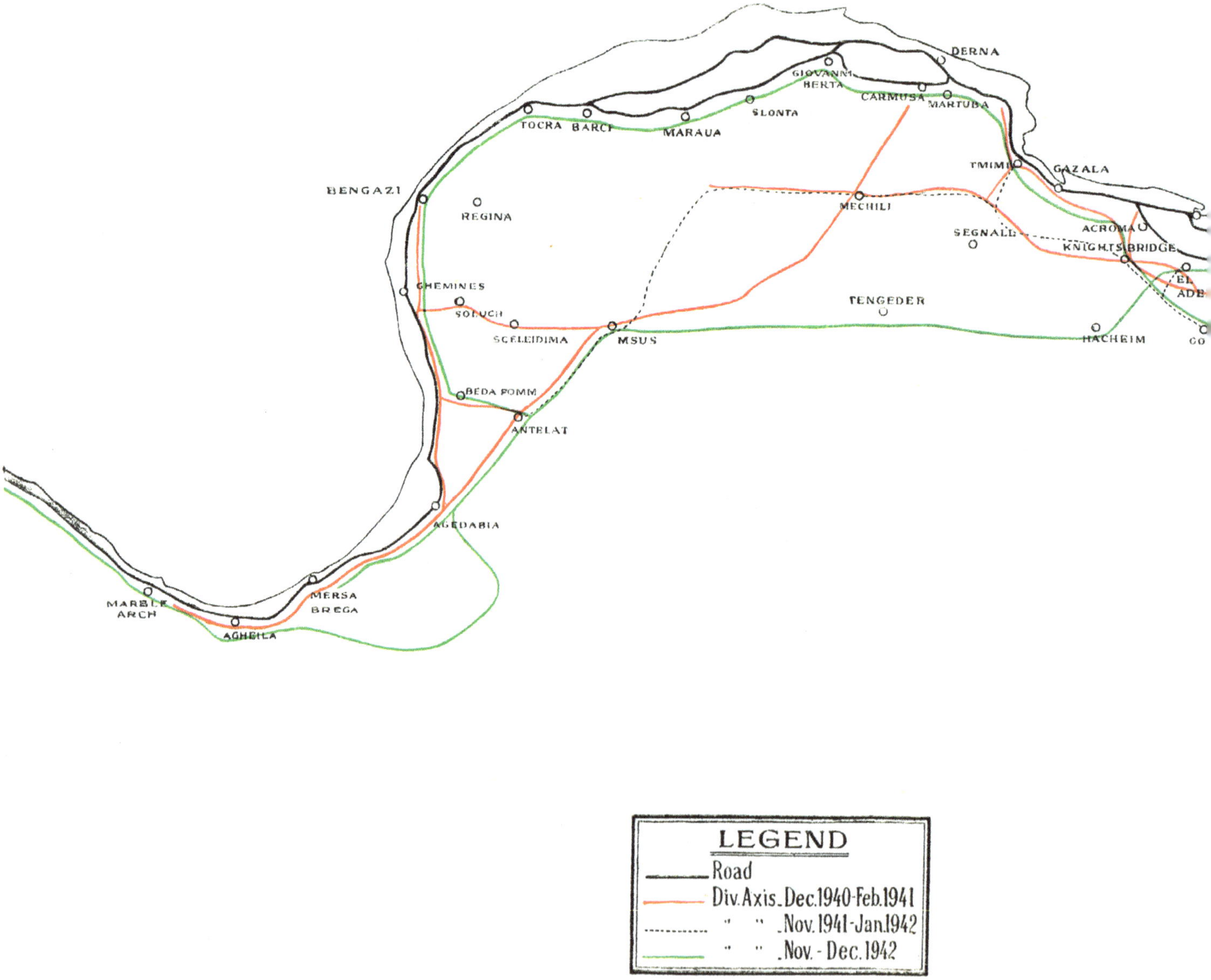

DERNA
GIOVANNI BERTA
CARMUSA
MARTUBA
SLONTA
MARAUA
BARCE
TOCRA
BENGAZI
REGINA
TMIMI
GAZALA
MECHILI
SEGNALI
ACROMA
KNIGHTSBRIDGE
TENGEDER
HACHEIM
GHEMINES
SOLUCH
SCELEIDIMA
MSUS
BEDA FOMM
ANTELAT
AGEDABIA
MERSA BREGA
MARBLE ARCH
AGHEILA
LEGEND
Road
Div. Axis_Dec.1940-Feb.1941
" " .Nov.1941-Jan.1942
" " .Nov.-Dec.1942

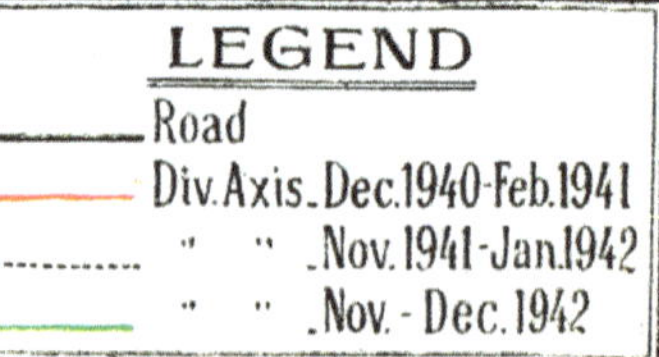

MAP II

ALEXANDRIA TO AGHEILA

SCALE. 1/2,000,000

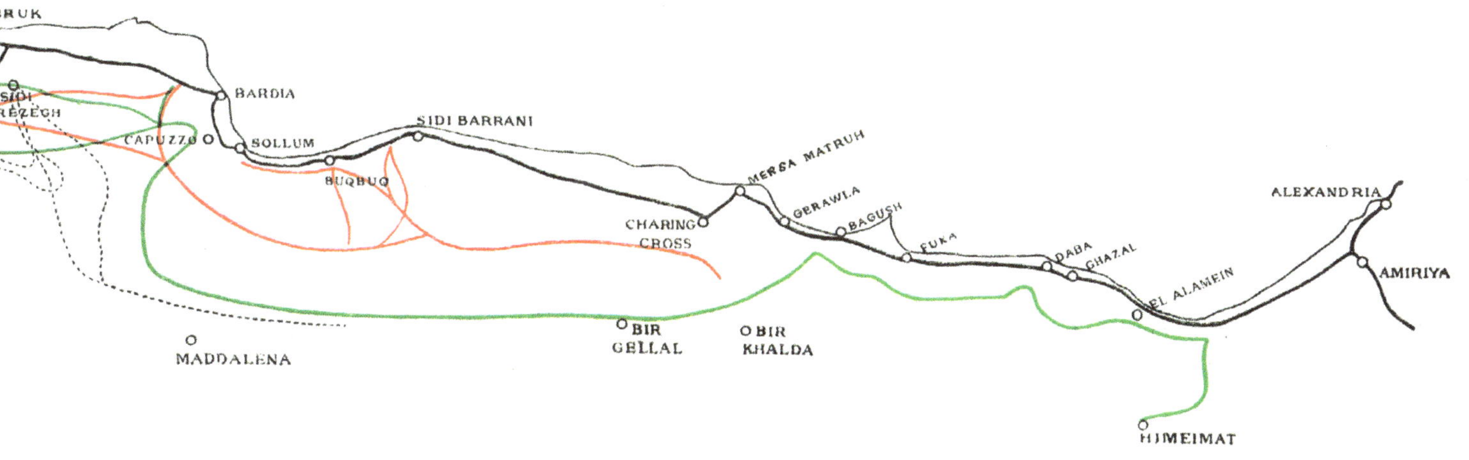

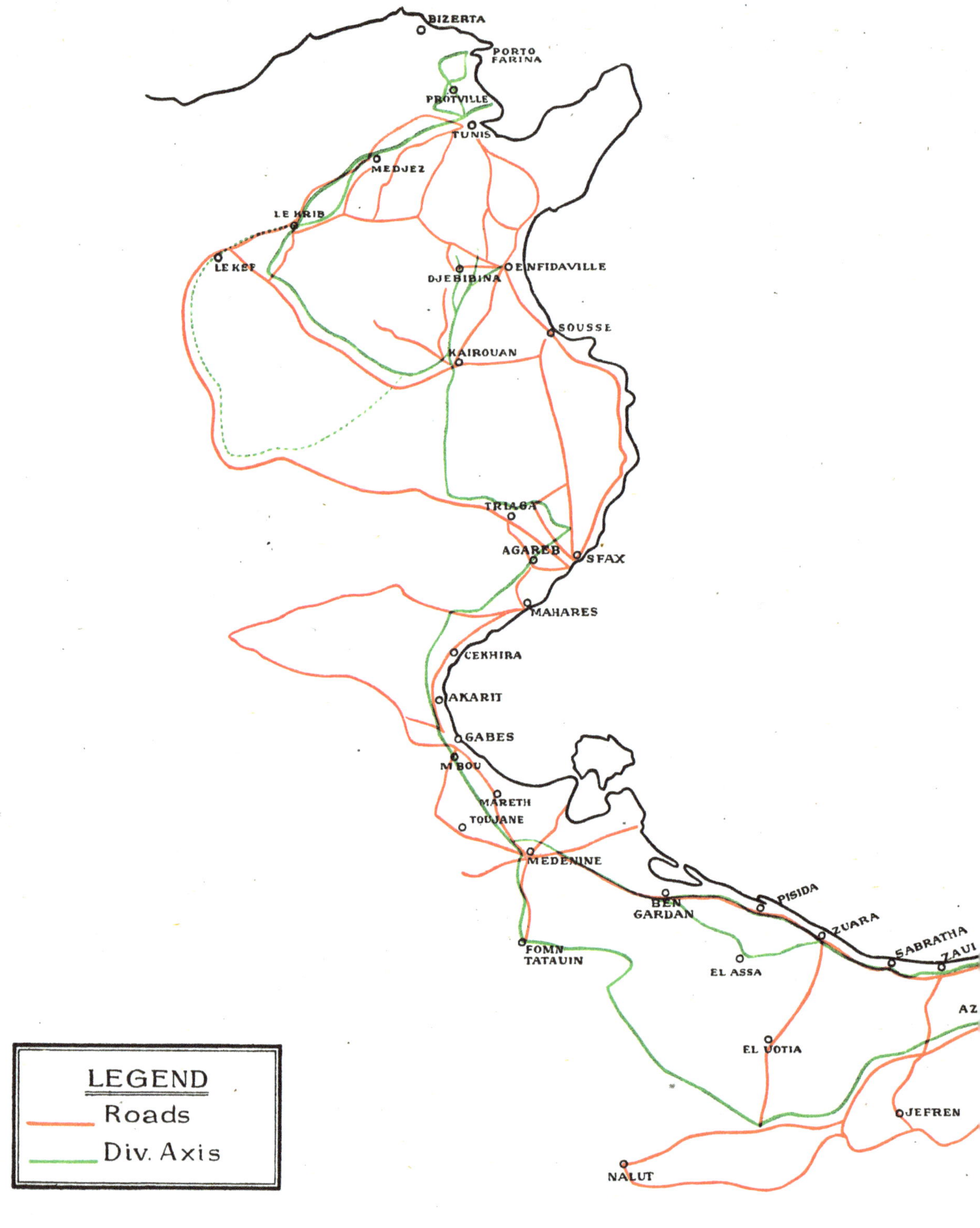
BIZERTA
PORTO FARINA
PROTVILLE
TUNIS
MEDJEZ
LE KRIB
LE KEF
DJEBIBINA
ENFIDAVILLE
SOUSSE
KAIROUAN
TRIAGA
AGAREB
SFAX
MAHARES
CEKHIRA
AKARIT
GABES
M BOU
MARETH
TOUJANE
MEDENINE
BEN GARDAN
PISIDA
ZUARA
SABRATHA
FOMN TATAUIN
EL ASSA
EL UOTIA
JEFREN
NALUT
LEGEND
Roads
Div. Axis

MAP III
NOFILIA TO TUNIS
SCALE 1/2,000,000

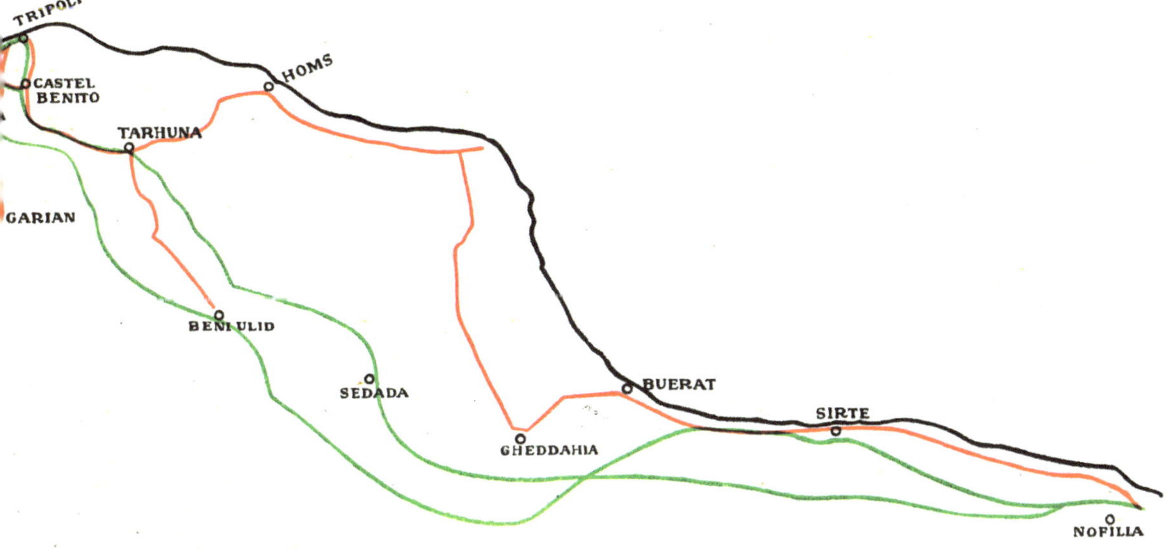

www.ingramcontent.com/pod-product-compliance
Lightning Source LLC
LaVergne TN
LVHW060620110826
845147LV00019B/1062

* 9 7 8 1 4 7 4 5 3 9 1 8 0 *